Make Friends with Your Impostor!

A Guide to Unlocking Your Hidden Superpower

Published by
Hybrid Global Publishing
333 E 14th Street
#3C
New York, NY 10003

Manufactured in the United States of America, or in the United Kingdom when distributed elsewhere.

Dickopf, Daphne
www.daphnedickopf.com
Make Friends With Your Impostor! A Guide to Unlocking Your Hidden Superpower
    ISBN: 978-1-961757-70-7
    eBook: 978-1-961757-69-1

Cover design by: Julia Kuris
Copyediting by: Sue Toth
Interior design by: Suba Murugan
Illustrations: Daphne Dickopf

To the 70% of us who have or will experience impostor feelings at one point in our lives.
To my husband who always supports me, encourages me, and believes that I can achieve anything that I want.
To my children who are my greatest teachers.

Acknowledgments

I am deeply grateful to my husband for encouraging me to write this book. To my family, thank you for your unwavering patience and understanding during the many hours I dedicated to this project. Your support has been invaluable, and I couldn't have completed this journey without your encouragement and love.

A heartfelt thank you to my friends and colleagues Corinne, Craig, Ildiko, Kerrie, and Vanessa. Your insightful feedback, steadfast support, and constructive criticism have been instrumental in shaping this book. Your contributions have made it more realistic, comprehensive, and impactful. I am truly fortunate to have you all by my side.

Also, thank you to all my friends who have held countless discussions with me about my book and the tools, even though most of you have never felt like an impostor. Your insights and discussions were incredibly helpful.

Thank you all for believing in me and for helping to bring this book to life.

Contents

A Note to the Reader

Welcome to this journey of conquering impostor feelings, making friends with them, unlocking your superpower, and reclaiming your confidence. I'm thrilled to share the stories and tools in this book with you, and I genuinely hope they will guide you towards a stronger, more self-assured you. Over the years, I've worked with countless individuals grappling with impostor feelings, and I've gathered a variety of tools that have proven effective for my clients – and for myself too.

In Part One, we explore the facts and figures behind the impostor phenomenon, laying the foundation for understanding what you're up against. In Part Two we look at how to use this book and examine the underlying premise – the groundwork needed to be able to work on changing the trajectory of impostor feelings. Part Three introduces a comprehensive framework – the Impostor Strategy Matrix™ – of the foundational elements needed to break the imposter cycle and of four key elements, designed to be your roadmap for transforming these feelings into newfound strength. In Part Four, you discover and apply forty practical tools aimed at managing, modifying, and transforming impostor feelings into a more productive path, boosting your self-confidence and self-worth. In Part Five, you will craft a personalized strategy tailored to your unique needs, helping you master your impostor feelings for good. Finally in Part Six you explore the next steps for the road ahead.

By following this structured approach, you'll unlock the potentia to overcome self-doubts and achieve personal and professional fulfillment. Together, we'll delve into intercepting triggers, providing first aid, establishing a sustainable support system, cultivating resilience, and shaping your vision for the future.

My wish is that the tools in this book will offer you a variety of ideas on how to regain control over your doubts and design a strategy to embrace your impostor feelings. I hope you'll come to see these feelings not as weaknesses, but as catalysts for unlocking your true strengths, your superpowers. Let's embark on this transformative journey together, turning impostor feelings into your greatest asset, and becoming the most confident person you can be.

My hope is, that one day in the not-too-distant future, talking about impostor feelings at home, school, the workplace, and at dinner parties will become the norm and sharing tools and methods how to support each other best to using these feelings to unlock the superpowers within us will be the new normal.

PART ONE

Introduction

From Impostor to Empowerment

Today, I have a job that truly makes me happy and fulfilled. I set ambitious goals to push myself just outside my comfort zone, collaborate with many talented leadership development professionals, and work with amazing leaders who have excelled in their respective fields. As an executive coach, leadership trainer, and management consultant specializing in individual, team, and organizational development, I engage with leading international companies, business schools, universities, and individual clients on a global scale.

What most people don't know about me is that I have felt like an impostor for as long as I can remember. I can't really pinpoint it to one specific cause. When I was young growing up in Switzerland, I had allergies from spring to fall each year resulting in asthma and thus had difficulties breathing. As a consequence, whenever I ran, I was immediately out of breath and had to use an inhaler to be able to breathe normally again. This meant I wasn't particularly good at sports and often got picked last when the kids had to choose their own teammates. When I would tell my mom about these moments, she would tell me that it wasn't important and sports didn't really matter—it was her way of trying to support me. This really didn't make me feel better—just more like someone who didn't belong, someone who wasn't good enough and couldn't compete with others on their level. I saw this repeated when I got a grade that was not as high as I would have

1

liked it. My mom would brush it off and say, "Don't worry, it's not important!" But it was important to me! I felt not good enough, like I was destined to fail again next time.

In Switzerland, after sixth grade kids can go into one of four different streams of secondary school. My teacher at the time made the recommendation for me to go to the second highest of those four levels. I remember feeling that I didn't belong there, that I was not smart enough and that it must have been luck or a mistake that I was sent there. This feeling that I was lucky when I got a good grade or when I passed exams continued throughout all my school and during my university studies.

After getting my bachelor's degree in the United Kingdom, my first job was as a management consultant at a renowned international management consultancy in Germany. In the 90s, university studies in most of continental Europe took much longer than today where most countries have aligned to the bachelor and master programs. As a result, when I started as a twenty-three-year old management consultant, I was more than five years younger than most of my peers at the consulting company. This prompted Thomas, my manager at the time, to approach me and tell me that I was not allowed to tell anyone on our client's team how young I was. Once again, I felt like I didn't belong, that my university degree was not enough. I tried to dress more conservatively to make myself look older, and I carefully selected my words to sound smarter.

During my ten years as a management consultant for three different firms, that feeling of not belonging and feeling like a fraud remained a constant. I believed I didn't belong because I wasn't as educated, as articulate, as analytical, as bold, or as aggressive as my peers. While I generally got really good performance reviews, I found elements in it that reinforced this feeling, pushing me to try harder, achieve more, and emulate my colleagues. It took years to realize that I had focused on the wrong aspects of my personality. Instead of honing my strengths – building relationships, motivating clients, and empathizing with their difficulties – I fixated on my weaknesses. I feared being exposed for my lack of proficiency, for example in Excel, overlooking the importance of my interpersonal skills, which I deemed merely "nice to have" in this job. I overestimated my weaknesses and underestimated my strengths, partly because I lacked the right role models in my environment.

Improving the areas highlighted in my performance reviews – such as data analysis, Excel proficiency, and consulting model development – felt incredibly challenging, as I had no passion for them. My true passion lay in building relationships with clients, helping them embrace and lead organizational change. According to both my clients and managers, I excelled in these areas, but my subjective view undervalued their significance.

Had I known at that time, that my feelings of inferiority were actually impostor feelings and that I could just confront them and implement strategies to manage them and grow confident, wow, that would have saved me a lot of time, tears, and worries! Instead, it was more gradual for me. I tried extra hard, tried to be bolder, tougher, and sometimes even more aggressive than my male colleagues, trying to always go the extra mile. This resulted in lots of late nights, weekends, sometimes having to cancel on my friends, and along the way somewhere forgetting what was really important to me.

As the situation became increasingly unbearable, I sought out development books and started my first coaching training which allowed me to focus on my own personal development. Through this journey, I discovered my first tools – some of which I will share in this book – fostering a vision for myself, building resilience, and managing my impostor feelings. This led me to rethink my priorities and make significant changes in my life. As one of the consequences, I left consulting and joined a business school in a leadership position to develop their executive education programs. There, I realized that with the right framework in place, I felt empowered, smart enough, articulate enough, tough enough, and capable. I began to recognize and coach others – employees, colleagues, and friends – who were grappling with impostor feelings. I noticed a pattern: people seemed to follow a process to transform their impostor feelings into their superpower.

In the years that followed, my fascination with the impostor phenomenon only deepened. I delved into understanding its triggers and identifying tools to intercept, manage, modify, and transform feelings of doubt into confidence. While I developed my own strategy to handle these feelings effectively, my work as an executive coach and leadership development specialist allowed me to guide countless clients through their struggles. Through hundreds of coaching sessions, I helped them devise personalized strategies to embrace their impostor feelings and achieve the success they desired.

Witnessing the transformation in my clients as they learned to navigate their own impostor challenges has been profoundly rewarding. Each individual's journey reinforced my belief that these tools and strategies could benefit a much broader audience. It became clear to me that the framework I developed could help many more people beyond my one-on-one coaching sessions. This realization inspired me to write this book.

By sharing these insights and tools, I hope to empower you to turn your impostor feelings from a source of self-doubt into a powerful force for growth and achievement. Together, we'll explore how to build lasting confidence, leverage your unique strengths, and create a fulfilling and successful professional life. Let's embark on this transformative journey, turning self-doubt into a superpower that propels you toward your dreams.

Have I completely overcome my impostor feelings? No, I don't believe it's possible to overcome them entirely. Every time a new challenge arises, my impostor feelings flare up, but now I have tools in place to manage them. I feel like an impostor much less often, and when I do, I no longer let those feelings dictate my actions or define my reality. I have learned to balance humility with confidence, recognize my strengths and passions, accept my flaws without self-criticism, and acknowledge my achievements without arrogance. I have embraced my impostor feelings and made friends with them.

Impostor Phenomenon

You might have come across the work of Pauline Rose Clance and Suzanne Imes, two therapists and professors from Georgia State University who coined the term "Impostor Phenomenon" in the late 1970s. They noticed that numerous women couldn't internalize their successes, believing instead that they were not genuinely competent. Despite all their achievements, these women felt like they weren't really cut out for their success. While they initially thought it was mostly a women's issue, newer studies have shown that men and women are equally susceptible.

The Impostor Phenomenon is a complex pattern that affects countless individuals, causing them to doubt their accomplishments and fear that others will expose them as frauds. Rooted deeply in the interplay between self-perception and external expectations, this phenomenon is not just about feeling like a fake but involves a persistent fear of not living up to one's own standards or those of others.

These days the impostor phenomenon is often referred to as "Impostor Syndrome." The term makes it sound like a medical condition. Originating from a medical context, "syndrome" suggests a set of symptoms characteristic of a particular disease, thereby implying that feeling like an impostor is a psychological disorder. However, as it is not a mental condition, it shouldn't be named as such. This is one of the reasons, that for the remainder of the book, I will not use the term impostor syndrome any longer but rather call it impostor phenomenon, impostor feelings, or the like.

Individuals experiencing impostor phenomenon often undergo what's known as the "Impostor Cycle." This cycle begins with doubt and worry, escalating to fear and anxiety which can lead to procrastination or excessive preparation. Upon completing a task, they might feel relief or pride, but these feelings are fleeting. Success is often dismissed as not truly earned or as a sign that the task wasn't actually challenging.

Dr. Pauline Rose Clance outlines specific traits that characterize those grappling with the impostor phenomenon.[1]

Dr. Clance identified six traits that are common among those who feel like impostors:

1. **Impostor Cycle**: The impostor cycle is characterized by an ongoing loop of self-doubt, over-preparation, and dismissive feelings following success. Individuals caught in this cycle often work excessively hard to ensure their performance meets their high standards. However, once they achieve success, they quickly dismiss it as unearned or attribute it to external factors, leading to persistent feelings of fraudulence and the need to prove themselves repeatedly.

2. **Need to be Special, to be the Very Best**: This trait involves a compulsion to be the best at everything, coupled with an inability to accept anything less than perfection. Individuals with this trait feel that they must always excel and be recognized as the top performer in any endeavor. This relentless pursuit of excellence often leads to chronic stress and disappointment when they inevitably fall short of their unattainable standards.

3. **Superwoman/Superman Aspects**: Perfectionism in every aspect of life defines this trait. Those exhibiting Superwoman/Superman aspects strive for perfection in all their roles, whether personal or professional. This perfectionism can lead to overwhelming stress and burnout when they are unable to meet their own high expectations. They feel the pressure to handle everything flawlessly, leaving little room for error or relaxation

4. **Fear of Failure:** A profound fear of failure drives this trait, where any mistake or shortcoming is perceived as a disaster. Individuals with this fear often avoid taking risks or trying new things due to the anxiety that any failure will confirm their inadequacy. This fear

---

[1] Adapted from Dr. Pauline Rose Clance, *The Impostor Phenomenon: Overcoming the Fear That Haunts Your Success* (Atlanta, GA: Peachtree Publishers, 1985), 25-28.

can paralyze their growth and prevent them from seizing opportunities that could lead to personal and professional development.

5. **Denial of Competence and Discounting Praise**: This trait involves an inability to accept personal success as valid, often attributing achievements to luck, timing, or deception. Individuals deny their own competence and frequently downplay their accomplishments, believing they do not deserve the praise they receive. This denial perpetuates feelings of being a fraud and makes it difficult for them to internalize their successes.

6. **Fear of and Guilt about Success**: Concerns that success might alienate peers or increase pressure and responsibilities define this trait. Individuals fear that their achievements will set them apart from others or lead to unrealistic expectations for future performance. They may feel guilty about their success, worrying that it could create envy or resentment among colleagues, friends, or family, thereby complicating their interpersonal relationships.

6 Common Traits

IMPOSTOR CYCLE
- ongoing loop of doubt and over-preparation
- possibility of procrastination
- dismissive feelings after success

BE SPECIAL - THE VERY BEST
- the need to be the best - number one
- inability to accept that they cannot remain the best
- feel stupid if they are not the very best

SUPERWOMAN / SUPERMAN
- perfectionism in every aspect
- significant successes feel like mere duties
- placing undue pressure on every new challenge

FEAR OF FAILURE
- any mistake amounts to a disaster
- avoiding risks or challenges
- can prevent from personal and professional growth

DENIAL OF COMPETENCE & DISCOUNTING PRAISE
- downplaying own achievements
- attributing success to luck or others' help
- failing to recognize or celebrate true capabilities

FEAR OF GUILT ABOUT SUCCESS
- leads to guilt and reluctance in self-promotion
- reinforced by cultural or familial emphasis on humility
- prevents from accepting and internalizing own achievements

On the basis of the concepts of Dr. Pauline Rose Clance

By understanding these traits, individuals can begin to recognize the patterns of impostor feelings and take steps to address and mitigate their impact on their personal and professional lives. According to Clance, people who have impostor feelings tend to have at least two of the above traits. Depending on how strong of impostor feelings someone has, they will be likely to have more of the above mentioned six traits. If you would like to know how pronounced you experience the impostor phenomenon, then the self-assessment – the Impostor Phenomenon Scale – developed by Dr. Clance is a helpful tool. You will find more information about this tool in the Appendix.

Further expanding on Clance's work and on her own research, Dr. Valerie Young categorized impostors into five types based on their specific behaviors and thoughts:[2]

1. **The Perfectionist**: Focuses on the flawless execution and outcome of tasks.
2. **The Expert**: Feels the need to know everything before starting a task, viewing any knowledge gap as a failure.
3. **The Soloist:** Believes they must accomplish tasks independently, viewing the need for help as a weakness.

5 Types of Impostors

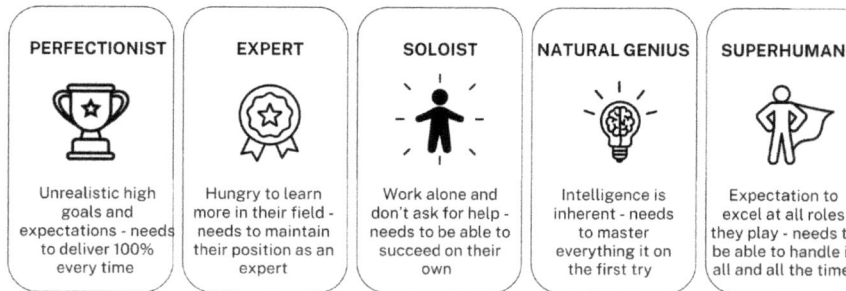

adapted from Dr. Pauline Rose Clance as well as Dr. Valerie Young

---

[2] Valerie Young, EdD, *The Secret Thoughts of Successful Women* (New York: Crown Currency, 2011), 108-135

4. **The Natural Genius**: Measures competence by how easily and quickly tasks are accomplished.
5. **The Superhuman**: Tries to excel in all roles they juggle, viewing any shortcoming as a personal failure.

You might say, but there is nothing wrong with being an expert and frankly, there isn't. However, when looking at the five types of impostors, keep in mind that the need to be a perfectionist, expert, soloist, natural genius or superhuman is not born out of excelling at something or just finding this the best way forward. Instead, it stems from a necessity to cover up the fear of others exposing you as a fraud, believing you have no clue what you are doing.

Addressing these patterns involves conscious efforts to recognize and adjust your internal narratives. This might mean practicing acceptance of praise and consciously reflecting on the individual contributions you made to achieve success. It also involves setting realistic and attainable goals, allowing yourself to fully appreciate and celebrate when you meet them. By redefining what success looks and feels like on a personal level, you can begin to dismantle the harmful effects of these tendencies and build a healthier, more positive self-image.

Understanding these patterns and categories helps illuminate why individuals might struggle to acknowledge their achievements and fee constant pressure to perform. By understanding that you might identify with one or more of these types, it is easier to begin to address your impostor feelings constructively. This knowledge not only demystifies the feelings of being an impostor but also provides a roadmap for personal growth and acceptance.

Impostor Coping Mechanism

People grappling with impostor phenomena often engage in unconscious behaviors to manage the anxiety of being "found out" and to avoid exposure. These coping mechanisms can provide temporary relief but often reinforce the cycle of self-doubt and anxiety. Here are the ten most common coping or protecting mechanisms:

1. **Holding Back:** Avoiding social situations where their competence might be judged. This behavior limits opportunities for growth and learning, and it can prevent individuals from fully participating in their personal and professional lives.
2. **Hard Work:** Putting in excessive effort, working long hours, and over-preparing to ensure they meet or exceed expectations. While this can lead to temporary success, it often results in burnout and reinforces the belief that they must always go above and beyond to prove their worth.
3. **Use of Charm:** Relying on charm to gain approval and divert attention from perceived inadequacies. This can create a superficial layer of confidence but prevents deeper connections and authentic self-expression.
4. **Procrastination:** Delaying tasks to avoid the fear of failure, providing an excuse if the outcome isn't perfect. This often leads to increased stress and rushed work, perpetuating a cycle of anxiety and self-doubt.
5. **Never Finishing:** Avoiding completion to escape judgment on their work. This can stall career progress and personal development, as unfinished tasks and projects accumulate, reinforcing the fear of failure.
6. **Never Starting:** Failing to begin projects due to fear of not meeting high standards. This can lead to missed opportunities and stagnation, as individuals avoid taking risks and trying new things.
7. **Validation**: Relying heavily on praise from others to feel competent and confirm their abilities. This external dependence undermines self-confidence and creates a constant need for reassurance.
8. **Avoiding Display of Confidence:** Downplaying skills to avoid being perceived as arrogant or to avoid scrutiny. This behavior can

prevent individuals from receiving recognition and opportunities they deserve, reinforcing their feelings of inadequacy.

9. **Minimizing Achievements:** Attributing success to luck or external factors rather than their own abilities, maintaining the belief they are not truly competent. This mindset devalues their hard work and accomplishments, hindering self-confidence and personal growth.

10. **Self-Sabotage:** Engaging in behaviors that undermine their success to maintain the belief they are not deserving of their achievements. This can include missing deadlines, underperforming, or not taking advantage of opportunities, which ultimately limits their potential and reinforces impostor feelings.

While these coping mechanisms can provide temporary relief, they ultimately reinforce the impostor phenomenon, perpetuating feelings of inadequacy and anxiety. Recognizing and addressing these behaviors is crucial for breaking the cycle and building a healthier, more confident self-image.

On the basis of Dr. Pauline Rose Clance as well as Dr. Valerie Young

You Are Not Alone

Ever felt like you're just not cut out for something, even when everyone else thinks you're doing great? That little voice that keeps bugging you with questions like, "Who am I to do this?" or "I am not as competent as everyone thinks." The reassuring truth is that you are not alone in your battle against your impostor feelings. It is a shared experience among many highly educated, intelligent, and successful individuals. In fact, it's more common than you might think.

The following studies that have been conducted in the past two decades show how prevalent the impostor phenomenon (IP) is and how this is true for various groups:

People reporting to have experienced IP

at one point in their lives

(Sakulku, 2011)

of female executives

(KPMG, 2020)

of members of ethnic minority groups

(Bravata, 2019)

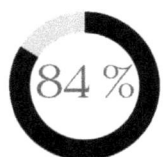

of female 1st year medical students

(Wrench, 2024)

According to a study in the International Journal of Behavioral Science back in 2011, about seventy percent[3] of us will feel like an impostor at some point. A more recent study by KPMG performed in 2020, revealed that "75 percent of female executives report having personally experienced Impostor Syndrome at certain points in their career."[4] That same study also found that communication and collaboration play a vital role in helping to reduce self-doubt and promote self-worth. Forty-seven percent of female executives identified having a supportive boss as the number one factor in the workplace to reduce impostor phenomenon. Twenty-eight percent identified feeling va ued and being rewarded fairly as integral to a positive work environment. Encouragement, understanding and recognition from leadership can also help to ward off Impostor feelings.

In 2019, Bravata[5] et al did a meta study analyzing 62 studies and they discovered that the IP was particularly high among ethnic minority groups – as high as eighty-two percent. This was topped by a recent study of female first year medical students in the US, where 84% had reported to have experienced IP[6].

Many famous people who have been feeling like a fraud have expressed their experience with IP. For example, the renowned poet and author Maya Angelou is a famous example of someone who experienced impostor phenomenon. She is quoted to have said, "I have written eleven books, but each time I think, 'Uh oh, they're going to find out now. I've run a game on everybody, and they're going to find me out.'"

---

[3] Jaruwan Sakulku, James Alexander, "The Impostor Phenomenon," *Internationa'
Journal of Behavioral Science*, 20˙ 1, Vol. 6, No.1, p.73-92.

[4] *Advancing the Future of Womer. in Business*, The 2020 KPMG Women's Leadership Summit Report, https://assets.kpmg.com/content/dam/kpmg/sk/pdf/2020/2020-KℲMG-Womens-Leadership-Summit-Report.pdf .

[5] Dena M. Bravata, Sharon A. Watts, Autumn L. Keefer, Divya K. Madhusudhan, Katie T. Taylor, Dani M. Clark, Ross S. Nelson, Kevin O. Cokley, and Heather K. Hagg, *Journal of General Internal Medicine*, Prevalence, Predictors, and Treatment of Impostor Syndrome: a Systematic Review, 2019; 35(4):1252–75

[6] Algevis Wrench, Maria Padilla, Chasity O'Malley, Arkene Levy, Heliyon, Impostor phenomenon: Prevalence among 1st year medical students and strategies for mitigation, Heliyon 10 (2024) e29478

Another very public figure who has been an advocate of speaking about what feeling like an impostor is former first lady Michelle Obama. She has openly talked about feeling like an impostor and how she "had to work to overcome that question that I always ask myself: am I good enough?".[7] The explanation about the impostor phenomenon from the actor Tom Hanks is "No matter what we've done, there comes a point where you think, 'How did I get here? When are they going to discover that I am, in fact, a fraud and take everything away from me?'"[8] These are just three of countless people who have had struggles with not feeling like they are good enough or did not deserve a seat at the table.

So, how do you know if the impostor phenomenon is something you should be concerned about? Everyone experiences some form of self-doubt from time to time, especially when attempting something new. But when does feeling like a fraud become more substantial, impacting your daily life? Impostor phenomenon often involves chronic self-doubt and insanely high self-expectations that go beyond occasional uncertainty. If these feelings persist and significantly influence your behavior, keeping you from taking risks or seizing opportunities, they may be more than just a cautionary mechanism, then chances are that you are grappling with impostorism.

If you find yourself consistently downplaying your achievements, fearing exposure as a fraud, or recognizing one or more of the common coping mechanisms associated with impostor phenomenon, it might be relevant to you. For a more precise assessment, consider taking the test provided at the end of this book in the appendix. This can help you gauge how pronounced your impostor feelings are and determine if they are affecting your life and success and the tools desired in this book will be a helping stepping stone to conquering your impostor feelings.

---

[7] Michelle Obama describes her battles with impostor syndrome, 2019: https://www.youtube.com/watch?v=5EP-ljBlf38
[8] Tom Hanks on self-doubt, 2026, https://www.npr.org/2016/04/26/475573489/tom-hanks-says-self-doubt-is-a-high-wire-act-that-we-all-walk

The Hidden Costs

The hidden costs of the impostor phenomenon go far beyond personal anxiety and self-doubt, significantly affecting individuals' professional lives and well-being. Those grappling with impostor feelings often experience reduced self-confidence, which manifests in several limiting behaviors. They might hold back from sharing innovative ideas, hesitate to ask critical questions, or avoid stepping up for challenging opportunities and assignments. Such behaviors can lead to missed promotions, silenced voices, and an overall stagnation in career progression.

The implications for personal growth are considerable. Individuals may over-personalize constructive feedback, procrastinate on important projects, and frequently change jobs in an attempt to escape feelings of fraudulence, inadvertently sabotaging their own success. This cycle of behavior can lead to overworking and over-preparation, ultimately

5 Most Commen Hidden Costs

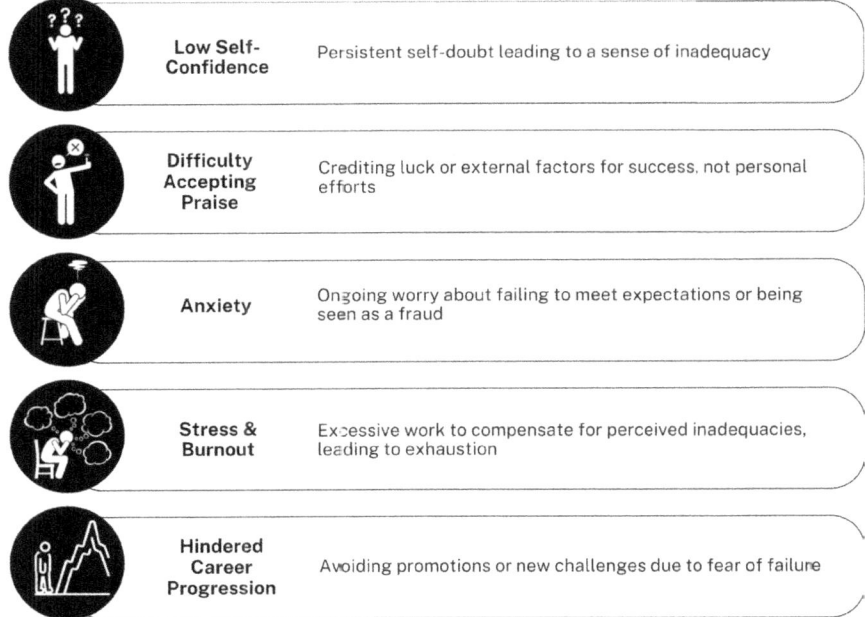

	Low Self-Confidence	Persistent self-doubt leading to a sense of inadequacy
	Difficulty Accepting Praise	Crediting luck or external factors for success, not personal efforts
	Anxiety	Ongoing worry about failing to meet expectations or being seen as a fraud
	Stress & Burnout	Excessive work to compensate for perceived inadequacies, leading to exhaustion
	Hindered Career Progression	Avoiding promotions or new challenges due to fear of failure

resulting in burnout, increased psychological stress, and fatigue. Such actions not only diminish an individual's performance and potential but also cost them financially–both in terms of missed salary increases and potential promotions.

If we look at this from a more tangible place, the financial impacts can be substantial. For instance, in 2020 Intuit Mint, a former personal financial management website and mobile app for the US and Canada, estimated that Americans who experience impostor phenomenon could be missing out on as much as $7,500 annually by not negotiating salaries or advancing in their careers due to self-doubt. This self-doubt can also lead to a constant job-hopping, which not only disrupts one's career trajectory but also might lead to longer periods of unemployment between jobs. Overcoming these impostor feelings is crucial not just for personal fulfillment but also for achieving long-term career success and financial stability.

If you look at these foregone costs over a working life, that is an immense amount. Let's assume you work 40 years and each year you forgo $7,500. Assuming you put it in a bank account without considering any interest rates, within 40 years, that amounts to $300,000. Now, let's assume the additional $7,500 each year over 40 years was invested at 5%; that amounts to roughly $900,000. At an interest rate

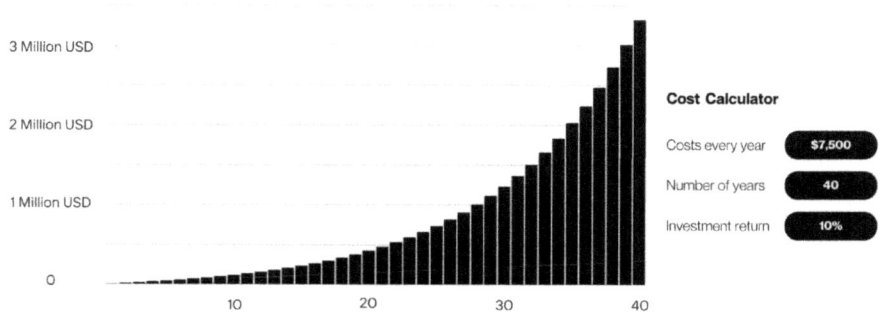

Forgone Costs of IP Over a Working Life

of 7%, it would have been $1,500,000, and at a 10% interest rate, $3,350,000. So, a really substantial loss if the impostor phenomenon has been holding you back from negotiating your salary or advancing your career.

The impostor phenomenon can carry significant hidden costs for companies as well. In 2020, Intuit Mint estimated that U.S. businesses lose about $3,400 annually in productivity per employee due to impostor feelings. Employees grappling with these feelings are less likely to speak up, take on challenges, or advocate for themselves, leading to missed opportunities and slower career advancement. This can result in procrastination, self-sabotage, and reluctance to seek promotions, often causing them to overwork and risk burnout. Additionally, these employees might spend excessive time on unnecessary upskilling or qualifications. For employers, this translates to higher turnover rates and the associated costs of hiring and training new employees. Overworking and overpreparing not only lead to wasted time but also reduce overall productivity, leading to fewer innovative ideas and solutions, lost opportunities, and a diminished talent pool.

The Impostor's Dilemma

Impostor phenomena is like a shadow lurking in the corners of our minds, affecting people from all walks of life, regardless of their achievements or qualifications. It thrives on self-doubt and has an uncanny ability to make us question our worthiness. The seasoned professional, the ambitious entrepreneur, the brilliant scientist, all grapple with the impostor's dilemma – the constant fear of being unmasked as a fraud.

The impostor phenomenon evolves as we progress in our careers and lives. It is not a static feeling but rather a dynamic force that rears its head when we step into the unknown or accept new challenges. As we climb the ladder of success, it often becomes more pronounced in situations that demand greater expertise or responsibility.

In this book we look at tools to manage and leverage that impostor from a well-known and feared adversary to a beloved challenger, enabler, and friend. We delve into practical strategies to manage this formidable adversary: The Impostor, when harnessed correctly, can unlock our superpowers. It keeps us humble, encourages ongoing learning, and fosters resilience. We explore how embracing this intrinsic self-doubt can propel us towards excellence, serving as a driving force in our personal and professional growth.

For my coaching clients, I focus on how impostor feelings impact them at the present and how it might influence their future trajectories. Working closely together, we concentrate on practical steps forward rather than dwelling on the origins of these feelings. We set goals, identify obstacles, devise strategies, and cultivate habits to empower my clients in embracing and leveraging their inner impostor feelings. It is mainly from the work with my clients, that I was able to derive the tools and strategies I am presenting in this book.

I have seen over and over examples of how, when done right and diligently, the impostor is not a foe to be defeated but a companion on our journey of self-discovery. With determination and self-compassion, we can transform impostor into a source of strength. We can use it to remind us that we are constantly evolving, learning, and growing. Through the challenges it presents, we find stepping stones to our continued success, turning the impostor into a loyal ally on the path to self-realization.

Your Success and Your Achievements

Chances are your journey bears a striking resemblance to mine and countless others who've grappled with their own impostor feelings. But here's the thing–we're all here, standing tall amidst our achievements, despite or maybe precisely because of those nagging doubts. It's that innate drive to go above and beyond, to overdeliver and under-promise, that sets us apart. You're the type to meticulously double-check your work, to never settle for mediocrity, and to relentlessly pursue learning, even when you've already reached great heights.

Perhaps you're quick to brush off your accomplishments as mere luck, choosing instead to remain modest and humble in the face of praise or even not believe the praise is sincere. And when faced with new challenges, you likely dive headfirst into preparation, leaving no stone unturned in your quest for excellence.

Yet, in the pursuit of perfection, you may find yourself grappling with impostor feelings. Sometimes, these feelings can lead to procrastination, to hesitate before taking action, and to doubt your own abilities. You may convince yourself that you never have enough knowledge or experience, that there's always more to learn and achieve before you can truly feel confident in your abilities. But here's the beauty of it all – your impostor feelings, far from being a hindrance, are actually the driving force behind your success. They keep you grounded, hungry for knowledge, and perpetually striving for improvement. So, the next time that voice whispers, "You're not good enough," remember this your impostor might just be the best thing that ever happened to you.

Embracing the Impostor Within

We're all wonderfully unique, and when it comes to navigating our inner doubts, there's no magic bullet that works for everyone. As someone who's worn many hats – management consultant, trainer, executive education professional, leadership coach, daughter, mother, wife – I've had the incredible opportunity to observe and work with and learn from a wide array of individuals.

Over the last decade, I've interacted with thousands of people across coaching sessions, workshops, trainings, parenting interactions, and more. I've seen firsthand the many faces of impostor phenomena – each instance with its own peculiar way of making folks feel diminished, less smart, or unfit for new challenges. Yet, I've also observed that turning this energy into a form of hidden genius often requires just the right tools and a well-chosen strategy.

But here's something else I've learned: customization is key. Strategies need to resonate with one's personal style, habits, and preferences to truly work. It's the only way we as individuals can genuinely accept our feelings of doubt, intercept those impostor feelings, and turn them into strengths.

This book isn't about quick fixes or one-size-fits-all answers, because the journey of my clients and my own journey has shown me that overcoming these feelings takes some work. Instead, see this book as a companion and workbook on your journey – a tool to help you discover what clicks for you and how to apply it effectively. It's a process, one that might take some time and effort. I've been on this path for many years myself, grappling with my own impostor whispers. Time and again, I've managed to unearth my superpower in the face of doubt, only to find those whispers creeping back in when faced with even bigger challenges. Each time, I either fall back on strategies that have worked in the past or scout for new ones to reveal my superpower anew. It's become clear to me that with every new challenge, the goalposts move further, prompting me to stretch even more, an endless testament to perpetual growth. I am guessing that you want to stop feeling like an impostor. I have been there but this is not as simple as that. How you feel will change last, you first have to stop thinking and behaving like an impostor.

My earnest hope is for everyone to see their feelings of doubt not as weaknesses, but as a stepping stone to the strengths they truly can be. This book aims to offer you a rich array of tools to explore and tailor to your unique journey. Let this book be your guide and companion as you learn to master your inner doubts, unlock your vast potential, and step into a new area of confidence!

Let's Recap

In Part One, we have discussed the origins, characteristics, and traits of impostorism, as well as the coping mechanisms and the hidden costs associated with it:

Origins and Research: Pauline Rose Clance and Suzanne Imes coined the term "Impostor Phenomenon" in the late 1970s, observing that many women felt undeserving of their successes. Initially thought to be a women's issue, newer studies reveal that men are equally affected.

Core Characteristics: The impostor phenomenon involves chronic self-doubt and a persistent fear of being exposed as a fraud, despite evident achievements. It manifests as an ongoing cycle of doubt, anxiety, and dismissive feelings after success.

Traits of Impostorism: Common traits include the Impostor Cycle, the need to be the best, perfectionism, fear of failure, denial of competence, and guilt about success. Individuals with impostor feelings typically exhibit at least two of these traits.

Coping Mechanisms: People with impostor feelings often engage in behaviors like over-preparing, procrastinating, self-sabotaging, and seeking validation to manage their anxiety. These actions provide temporary relief but reinforce the cycle of self-doubt and anxiety.

Hidden Costs: The impostor phenomenon can lead to significant personal and professional costs, including reduced self-confidence, missed opportunities, job-hopping, burnout, and financial losses due to not negotiating salaries or advancing careers.

Understanding these patterns and categories helps illuminate why individuals suffering from impostor phenomena struggle to acknowledge their achievements and feel constant pressure to perform. This knowledge demystifies the feelings of being an impostor and provides a roadmap for personal growth and acceptance.

PART TWO

How to Use This Book

Part Two is dedicated to guiding you on how to effectively utilize this book to conquer impostor feelings and harness them to regain your confidence. In this chapter, we lay the groundwork for your journey by introducing a comprehensive framework comprising three foundational blocks and four engagement windows to effectively tackle your handle your impostor tendencies. The framework serves as your roadmap for navigating impostor phenomenon and transforming it into a new-found source of strength. In the following chapters, you'll uncover, evaluate, and apply various tools tailored to your individual needs, ultimately crafting a personalized strategy for mastering your impostor feelings. By following this structured approach, you'll unlock the potential to overcome self-doubt and achieve personal and professional fulfillment. Get ready to dive deep into the process of intercepting triggers, providing first aid, establishing a sustainable support system, cultivating resilience, and shaping your vision for the future. Let's embark on this transformative journey together, turning impostor feelings into your greatest asset to regaining your confidence.

Impostor Strategy Framework™

The Impostor Strategy Framework™, which I have developed after extensive experience guiding clients through their imposter struggles,

23

provides a clear structure to dealing with imposter feelings and offers a comprehensive guide to unlocking your hidden superpowers. Think of the framework like a house: at its foundation there are three blocks that ensure its stability, and at its core there are four windows – the engagement areas – relevant to engage with the different facets of impostor phenomenon. Both the foundational blocks as well as the engagement areas are needed to effectively turn impostor feelings into a source of strength and new found confidence. As is true for any foundation of a house it needs to be solid and stable and this holds true for this framework as well, the three foundational blocks are a must-have before you can focus on any tools or strategy. The windows of a house are all there for you to look through; however, you choose which of the windows to look through depending what you would like to see. The foundational blocks are essential to break the impostor cycle and thus a prerequisite to the 4 engagement windows which provide relevant tools to manage, embrace, modify, and transform impostor feelings.

At the beginning of Part Three, and then throughout Part Four for each of the quadrants of the Impostor Strategy Matrix™, I will begin

Impostor Strategy Framework™

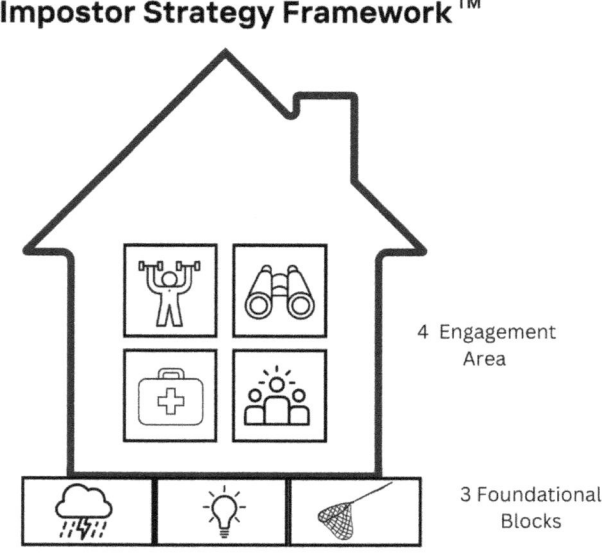

4 Engagement Area

3 Foundational Blocks

with a short client story, illustrating how they have used the tools described to address their impostor feelings and unlock their hidden superpowers. For confidentiality, I have changed the names of my clients, but their experiences and journeys remain authentic examples of how these tools can transform impostor feelings into superpowers.

Let's first look at the three foundational blocks needed to break the impostor cycle:

- Trigger
- Awareness
- Intervention

Trigger: This involves identifying what triggers your impostor feelings and promptly halting the cycle of negative self-talk and doubt every time they arise. It's like your brain is hitting a panic button called an "amygdala hijack," with fear suddenly in the driver's seat – what is also called the impostor cycle. Dr. Pauline Rose Clance observed that breaking the impostor cycle is essential for individuals to function optimally and embrace their achievements with confidence.[9] Understanding these triggers empowers you to intercept the thoughts as they arise, gaining control over your inner narrative and preventing further spiraling.

---

[9] Clance, *The Impostor Phenomenon*, 53.

Awareness: Once you know what your triggers are, then you start becoming aware of when impostor feelings take over your thoughts or decision-making process and what triggers them, whether it's certain situations, people, or challenges like speaking up in meetings or public speaking. Now that you know what can trigger it, the next step is to become aware of when the impostor cycle is starting. What we mean by that is that before you are entirely immersed in feeling like an impostor, become aware that and when these feelings start to manifest. It takes some practice to notice the onset of impostor feelings arising.

Intervention: There needs to be some kind of intervention in the impostor cycle which is a prerequisite to being able to prevent the cycle from taking its course and you feeling like a fraud. Only then can you break the impostor cycle, which is the single item needed before we can look at any tools on how to manage, embrace, modify, or transform impostor feelings.

In Part Three of this book, I will describe the practices needed for the foundational blocks. There are different ways to approach them but the importance is that they are foundational – they are the necessary groundwork needed before you can design your personal impostor strategy.

Now let's look at the four engagement windows:

At the core of the framework needed to embrace impostor feelings lies a potent matrix: the Impostor Strategy Matrix™. This 2x2 grid serves as your compass in finding the relevant tools for the four pillars to navigate these complex emotions. Tools are categorized based on their temporal impact, distinguishing between short-term and long-term solutions as well as efforts, which are classified by focus, delineating between internal introspection and external interactions.

To truly master and make peace with our impostor feelings, it's crucial to equip ourselves with a balanced toolkit across all four quadrants of this matrix. While many of us naturally gravitate towards one particular quadrant as our comfort zone, achieving personal growth often requires that we venture beyond, integrating tools from each quadrant into our strategy as well as including tools which are slightly more challenging for us. This section of the book will guide you through each quadrant, offering a detailed exploration of the al the tools within them. From quick internal shifts in mindset to long-term external supports, you'll discover how to build a comprehensive toolkit that not only helps you manage impostor feelings but also turns them into a source of strength and empowerment. By fostering balance and versatility in our approach, you can navigate your impostor feelings with grace and confidence.

Impostor Strategy Matrix ™

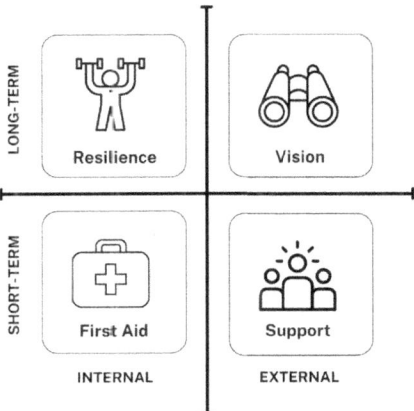

27

Explore, Pick, and Choose

As you dive into this book, think of it as a personalized roadmap through the Impostor Strategy Matrix™. Each quadrant is packed with tools designed to equip you with the capabilities you need to harness your impostor feelings. You're invited to explore all the tools across the four quadrants, but here's the kicker: if you already feel confident in one area, feel free to skip ahead to the sections that cover new or challenging territories for you. This approach ensures that you're not just going through the motions but actively engaging with tools that can make a real difference in your journey.

The tools are distributed across four quadrants: First Aid, Resilience, Vision, and Support. Each quadrant serves a distinct purpose for impostor feelings, from reshaping your self-perception to building up long-term resilience. When navigating through the tools of the four quadrants of the Impostor Strategy Matrix™, you might notice some tools may seem similar or related. This is intentional and shouldn't be a concern. They were created to address different aspects of the impostor experience or to function optimally under different circumstances. This design allows you to tailor your personal toolkit to suit your specific needs and preferences.

The true essence of this approach lies in its balance. It's recommended that you experiment with various tools and select at least three from each quadrant that resonate most with you. This personalized approach ensures that you are equipped with a versatile and effective set of strategies. By choosing tools that you find most helpful, you create a customized method to bolster your resilience against impostor feelings. Each element serves as a pivotal milestone towards mastering impostor feelings and unlocking your full potential. It is essential that you embrace all areas for sustainable short- and long-term success of becoming best friends with those impostor feelings of yours.

Remember, the goal here isn't to master every single tool but to build a personalized arsenal that you're comfortable and confident using. Over time, you'll find that these tools not only help manage impostor feelings but also enhance your overall self-confidence and personal growth.

For each tool, I've broken down the essentials:

- What it is
- Why it's important
- How to implement it
- When it's most effective

This clear, straightforward format is designed to help you quickly grasp the essence of each tool, making it easier to apply them to your life.

At the end of each tool's description, you'll find a reflective box asking two critical questions: What is the impact of this tool for me? (low, medium, high) and What is the effort required to implement the tool? (low, medium, high). These questions are your checkpoint, a moment to pause and assess the tool's relevance and feasibility for your personal situation. By actively evaluating each tool, you tailor the matrix to your needs, ensuring that your journey through the book is as impactful and efficient as possible. This book isn't just a collection of tools; it's a dynamic toolkit that adapts to your growth and challenges in embracing your impostor feelings. As you read through the tools and experiment with them, for every tool do a quick assessment of the impact this tool has for you and the effort required for you.

TOOL	LOW	MEDIUM	HIGH
Impact of this tool for me			
Effort required to implement tool			

In "Deriving Your Own Strategy," we will consolidate all the insights with the objective of equipping you with a comprehensive toolkit. The goal is for you to have at least three tools in each quadrant of the

Impostor Strategy Matrix™. By achieving this, you'll ensure that you possess the necessary resources to effectively manage, sustain, modify, and ultimately transform your impostor feelings.

Embracing the tools in your own strategy is not a one-time effort. It's an ongoing practice, a dynamic dance with your inner self. As you start to climb to new heights, face more daring challenges, and set loftier goals, those familiar impostor whispers may echo once again. Yet, this isn't a setback but a sign of progress, an opportunity to apply these steps with the finesse and intuition developed through practice. Each iteration not only makes the journey smoother but also deepens your relationship with yourself, turning what once felt like a daunting adversary into a trusted ally. As you integrate these steps into the fabric of your being, they become second nature, guiding you effortlessly towards embracing your full potential with confidence and grace. Remember, mastering your impostor feelings isn't about silencing them forever but learning to harmonize their voice with your own, transforming every whisper of doubt into a powerful chorus of self-assurance and resilience!

PART THREE

Tools to Break the Impostor Cycle

Carla, an accomplished HR professional at a US-based consulting firm, grappled with impostor voices for as long as she could remember. When we began our coaching sessions, Carla expressed feeling stagnant and lacking inspiration. She sought guidance to identify her areas for growth and engage in a purposeful pursuit of self-improvement. Specifically, she aimed to cultivate confidence, discover her authentic leadership style, and elevate herself to the role of a trusted advisor.

Despite a track record of consistent promotions every 2-3 years, Carla had doubts about her worthiness and qualification for her current position. When she compared herself with her peers, she thought that she didn't really deserve a seat at the table but that she should sit at the proverbial kids' table. She couldn't enjoy that she was part of the top management now, as she spent most of her time doubting herself. One of her mentors in the company, her senior by many years, was now a peer and Carla just felt inferior to him. In meetings, particularly with older, male colleagues, Carla experienced a sense of exclusion and inadequacy, triggering impostor feelings. These moments paralyzed her with the fear that she would soon be exposed as a fraud and she realized that it was something within her that was triggered.

During our coaching sessions, we focused on the three foundational pillars of trigger, awareness, and intervention. Carla identified the triggers that promted her impostor hijack: instances where she thought that she should sit at the kids' table, conversations that left her feeling excluded, and comments from her employees that undermined her sense of value. She learned to become aware of the physical cues of the anxiety in her body, such as tension in her throat and neck, and practiced a quick body scan followed by focused breathing to reset herself in moments of stress. By intercepting the impostor hijack and reframing her response, Carla found she could navigate challenging situations with greater composure and without burning any bridges in the process.

In the weeks that followed, Carla diligently applied a three-step routine: that, where, what: noticing that something is going on, scanning her body, and identifying the negative self-narrative. This deliberate practice enabled her to interrupt her automatic reactions and regain control over her thoughts and actions. Through this process, Carla realized that succumbing to her impostor feelings only fueled irrationality, aggression, and self-doubt. By embracing self-awareness and implementing intercepting strategies, she reclaimed agency over her narrative and embraced a mindset of continuous improvement.

Carla's journey underscored the transformative power of intercepting impostor feelings. By acknowledging and addressing these challenges, she discovered newfound resilience and self-acceptance, paving the way for personal and professional growth.

In the journey of harnessing your impostor feelings, the first vital step is to break the impostor cycle. The following section points to the importance of identifying the triggers that set off a spiral of self-doubts and fear, develop your awareness to find that sweet spot just before the onset of the "impostor hijack", and practice effective interventions. It's about tuning in to your inner alarm system and recognizing the moments when your confidence begins to waver. Only when you learn to discern the early signs of impostor feelings will you be able to preemptively address these emotions before they escalate. Embrace this step as your foundation for transformation, setting the stage for a journey of empowerment and self-discovery.

Impostor Cycle: The Hijacking

Think of impostor feelings like a hijacking – a force taking over your thoughts, emotions, and actions, dictating your perception of yourself and your abilities. Intercepting these feelings requires a deep understanding of their triggers, timing, and tactics. Without an intervention, the cycle unfolds:

Trigger → Hijack → Surrender

In this sequence – without an interception – the impostor feelings intensify, doubting your abilities and eroding your confidence. The end result? A successful hijacking where you find yourself surrendering to these overwhelming feelings, feeling more like a fraud and less capable.

Imagine your brain undergoing an "amygdala hijack," where your fear response mechanism takes control. This primal reaction can overwhelm rational thinking, leading to a cascade of negative emotions and self-doubt. I call this the impostor hijack or simply impostor feelings. It's as if your will is seized, a takeover of your feelings and a domination of what you are allowed to do, dictated by these invasive thoughts.

However, there is a way to redirect this process – what we also call the three foundational blocks of the impostor Strategy Framework™ – in order to prevent the impostor hijack from taking place:

Trigger → Awareness → Intervention

1. **Triggers:** Identifying triggers is about closely observing the situations and environments that prompt feelings of being an impostor and toward reclaiming control.
2. **Awareness:** Developing awareness involves cultivating a keen sense of self-observation.

3. **Intervention**: Effective intervention requires a set of predetermined actions that you can deploy when you detect the onset of impostor feelings.

Dr. Pauline Rose Clance observed that the impostor cycle prevents people from being really successful and breaking the cycle is essential for individuals to function optimally and embrace their achievements with confidence.[10] By intercepting impostor feelings, you pave the way for personal growth, self-empowerment, and fulfillment. By systematically addressing triggers, honing your awareness, and practicing effective interventions, you gradually shift from a state of self-doubt to one of empowered self-assurance.

Let's explore the three foundational elements to manage your response to a impostor hijack by identifying triggers, developing awareness, and define effective interventions.

---

[10] Clance, *The Impostor Phenomenon*, 49

Identify Triggers

To know and understand what triggers your impostor hijack is crucial. Think of it like first knowing your ABC's before you can start writing words or even whole sentences. Only if you are really good at identifying each letter can you then move on to reading and spelling first easy and then ever more complex words. The same is true for the triggers, you need to get to know them from all angles, really becoming familiar what the nuances and specifics are that makes them come to light.

Some of the things that can get you triggered might be deeply ingrained in the way you think. They might be part of a very old limiting beliefs that you have – maybe since childhood. While it might be interesting to know exactly how you came to believe that, for the sake of working on transforming your impostor phenomenon to a newfound source of confidence. the semantics of that are not important. However, what is important is that you become really familiar with your limiting beliefs and then recognize them in the different forms they might manifest themselves.

Here is a short example what some of your limiting beliefs might be:

Limiting Belief
I am not intelligent enough
I am a fraud
I am not qualified enough

Now what triggers these feelings? Do these feelings surface during high-stakes meetings, when you're about to present your ideas, or perhaps when receiving feedback? Is it when you feel someone is not listening to you or is it when you have just had a success or received some kind of recognition? Document these triggers over time to discern patterns. Understanding these triggers is crucial as it prepares you to preemptively address the feelings before they escalate. Reflect on how these situations make you feel, the thoughts they provoke, and why they might be impacting you in this way.

To begin with you will most likely be able to identify and document your triggers after an impostor hijack has taken place. But this is a good start, now you at least become acquainted with what triggers your impostor feelings. Recognizing and identifying these triggers is the first step for breaking the cycle

My Notes on Triggers:

_____

_____

_____

_____

_____

_____

_____

_____

_____

_____

_____

_____

Train Your Awareness

The second foundational b ock is your awareness of when you are triggered. Pay attention not just to what triggers your impostor feelings, but also to how your body and mind react to these triggers. The physical sensations that people feel is different for each person. for example:

- Feeling a knot in the stomach
- Increasing heart rate
- Starting to sweat

What are the physical sensations that you are becoming aware of? Next time you are triggered and can feel an impostor hijack taking place, notice your physical sensations.

Once you have become aware of what physical sensations show the onset of impostor feelings rising, listen to the narrative about your capacities that you are telling yourself in these moments. This is also what is called automatic negative thoughts – or ANTs – where we feel like we've lost control of our own thoughts. A kind of negative self-talk that fills us with anxiety, guilt, and other negative emotions. They appear immediately in response to a trigger and are usually messages or fears that we have internalized for years.

Here is an example of what automatic negative thoughts could be with respect to our limiting beliefs:

Limiting Belief	Automatic Negative Thoughts (ANTs)
I am not intelligent enough	I can't speak up in the meeting because everyone will think that my ideas are stupid
I am a fraud	If I work hard to please everyone, they won't find out that I'm a fraud
I am not qualified enough	I can't apply for the higher position because everyone will find out that I'm not qualified enough

Becoming aware and noticing these signs – both physical sensations and automatic negative thoughts – early on can serve as a cue to implement your coping strategies. Additionally, this stage calls for emotional intelligence; recognizing the feelings without judgment and understanding they are not an accurate reflection of your reality or abilities. This mindful awareness creates a psychological buffer against the immediate impact of the impostor feelings.

My Notes on Awareness:

_____

_____

_____

_____

_____

_____

_____

_____

_____

_____

_____

Intercept the Impostor Hijack

The third foundational block puts a deliberate pause on the course of action of what would normally have resulted in an impostor hijack: a brief pause for you to consciously choose not to succumb to the impostor hijack. Deliberately intercept the onset of impostor feelings to disrupt the cycle. The goal is to interrupt the emotional and physiological responses that are being triggered – reactions that have likely become automatic over time and that we may not even realize we've grown accustomed to.

Next time you feel an impostor hijack about to happen – and you have become aware of the physical sensations and automatic negative thought patterns – try to intercept the hijack from taking place immediately. Trying to delay it for a few seconds while you become conscious of what is about to happen might be all that will be possible in the first few times.

Over time, these interventions can become reflexive responses that allow you to regain control over the situation. Gradually you will be able to prolong that pause, long enough to redirect your thoughts and your course of actions to choose another outcome. This is when you choose how to react rather than where your fear responses of your amygdala controls how you react. When you do, you will feel that you are back in control over your emotions and reactions.

By repeatedly practicing interventions, they become stronger, more automatic responses that can significantly dilute the power of impostor feelings over time. The key here is to create a mental space that allows you to reassess the situation from a place of strength and calm, not panic. Then you will be able to apply one of the tools from Chapter Four: Provide First Aid.

This is challenging work, so don't be discouraged if you don't succeed right away; it takes time and practice.

My Notes on Intercept:

_____

_____

_____

_____

_____

_____

_____

_____

_____

_____

_____

_____

_____

_____

Breaking the Impostor Cycle: Let's Recap

In this chapter, we explored the foundational elements of identifying and managing impostor feelings: triggers, awareness, and interception. Here's a summary of the key points:

Triggers

- **Identify Triggers:** Recognize specific situations or circumstances that provoke your impostor feelings, such as high-stakes meetings, presentations, or receiving feedback.
- **Document Patterns:** Keep track of when these feelings arise to discern patterns and better understand what triggers them.
- **Understand Limiting Beliefs:** Acknowledge underlying beliefs that fuel these feelings, like "I am not intelligent enough" or "I am a fraud."

Awareness

- **Physical Sensations:** Notice physical signs that indicate an impostor hijack is occurring, such as a knot in the stomach, increased heart rate, or sweating.
- **Automatic Negative Thoughts (ANTs):** Identify the negative self-talk that accompanies these triggers, which often includes irrational fears and doubts.
- **Emotional Intelligence:** Recognize and accept these feelings without judgment, understanding that they are not accurate reflections of your abilities.

Interception

- **Deliberate Pause:** Learn to consciously interrupt the onset of impostor feelings by creating a brief pause to regain control.

- **Prolonged Interventions:** With practice, extend these pauses to redirect your thoughts and actions, choosing a different, more constructive response.
- **Build Reflexive Responses:** Develop automatic responses to these feelings that help you maintain control and assess situations from a place of strength and calm.

By mastering these three foundational elements, you will have built a strong foundation required to effectively manage and mitigate the impact of impostor feelings.

In Part Four we will look at the four engagement windows – Provide First Aid, Cultivate Your Resilience, Shape Your Vision, and Establish a Support System – exploring ten tools each which can be helpful on your journey to embrace those impostor feelings as the powerful catalyst that they can be. The aim is not only to manage your impostor feelings during an active hijack but also to prepare yourself to sustain, modify, and finally transform these impostor feelings to a powerful ally to reclaim your confidence and unlock your superpowers.

PART FOUR
Tools to Embrace Your Impostor

In Part Four we will bring our attention to the engagement windows of the Impostor Strategy Framework™ by exploring each of the four engagement areas: Provide First Aid, Cultivate Your Resilience, Shape Your Vision, and Establish a Support System. You will recall that for each quadrant, the tools are grouped by two factors: their timeline (short-term or long-term impact) and their focus (internal reflection or external actions and resources).

For each quadrant I will explain how one of my coaching clients has tackled their impostor feelings with regards to that category. Then I will introduce ten tools that support that category, and finally at the end of each section, you will find a summary of those tools.

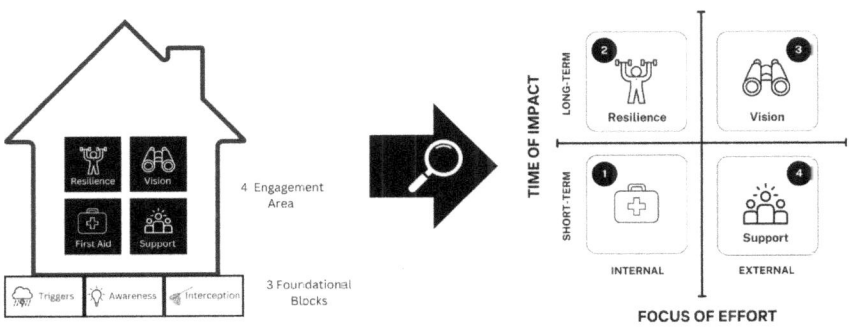

Each of the four quadrants of the matrix is equally important, however, each of the quadrants has a different focus:

1. **Provide First Aid**: Once you are aware that impostor feelings arise you now need to administer "first aid" by managing your emotional response. This is about employing techniques that are reframing negative thoughts and address the immediate impact. It's about regaining control over moments when you feel hijacked by your impostor feelings and turning them around

2. **Cultivate Your Resilience**: Developing resilience is key for harnessing impostor feelings as a source of strength. Understanding that gradually exposing yourself to challenges and setbacks as well as systematically learning from mistakes builds resilience, enabling you to bounce back stronger with each experience and navigate future obstacles with greater ease.

3. **Shape Your Vision**: Envisioning your desired future and aligning your actions with your goals propels you toward success. Embracing your impostor feelings as catalysts for growth allows you to transform your trajectory and realize your full potential. By acknowledging the role impostor feelings played in your successes, achievements aswell as your failures and forgone opportunities, you begin to experience their transformation into your superpower. Reframe your feelings and think like a non-impostor, embracing all that you are and can be.

4. **Establish a Support System**: Construct a sturdy support system, incorporating both human connections and practical habits tailored to building up your courage and stretching you out of your comfort zone. Nurturing this sustainable system ensures continual support and resources for navigating impostor feelings in the long haul. From trusted friends, mentors, and accountability partners to systematic habits and personalized resources, this empowers you to effectively manage and embrace your impostor in the long run.

When combining some tools from all four quadrants, you can create the perfect strategy for yourself to embrace your impostor. We will discuss this step in more detail in Part Five of this book.

Quadrant 1: Provide First Aid

Nathalie is a Senior Manager at a leading global management consulting firm in the Netherlands. At the outset of our work together, she had been recently passed over for a promotion from Manager to Senior Manager. She had long work weeks of 60-70 hours and she felt undervalued by her peers and superiors, often tasked with "housekeeping" duties like creating PowerPoint presentations, which she believed should fall to more junior staff.

Nathalie recognized that her reactions in these moments were driven by impostor voices, leaving her feeling irrational and out of control. We focused on techniques for her to regain her composure once these impostor voices emerged, employing tools such as self-compassion, embodiment practices, mindfulness, distinguishing facts from emotions, and humor – focusing mainly on the first quadrant: providing first aid.

Adopting this new perspective, Nathalie learned to slow down and examine her internal responses–both physical and mental–when triggered. She discovered that many situations weren't as dire as they seemed once she separated her impostor-driven emotions from the facts. With another promotion cycle approaching in six months, Nathalie chose to view her situation with gratitude for her health, the opportunity for advancement, and the guidance received from her mentor. Prepared and informed by her previous experiences, she focused on mindfulness and positive affirmation during interactions that previously would have triggered her impostor feelings.

An important aspect of Nathalie's growth was her commitment to being a good leader for her team. She recognized the importance of bringing her expertise to the table while ensuring her team had the freedom to develop and be creative in their approaches. This leadership style not only helped her team thrive but also contributed to her own professional development and sense of fulfillment.

This journey of self-improvement also led her to reevaluate her personal and professional relationships, seeking environments where she felt valued, supported, and challenged. Nathalie decided to make significant changes in her personal and professional life, specifically in her marriage and relationship with her boss.

The subsequent months were a blend of liberation, challenges, and hard work, culminating in her successful promotion to Senior Manager. This achievement marked a turning point for Nathalie, boosting her confidence and fearlessness towards future challenges. It also inspired her to redefine her personal expression through hobbies, wardrobe choices, and openly sharing her thoughts, reflecting her newfound self-assurance and place within the team.

The tools in this chapter focus on the first quadrant of the Impostor Strategy Matrix™. Once you have intercepted and reframed your impostor feelings, each tool is designed to help you move forward intentionally. This section is dedicated to addressing and soothing the immediate emotional upheaval caused by impostor feelings. Imagine being equipped with a mental first-aid kit, ready to deploy compassion, mindfulness, and cognitive reframing at a moment's notice. Here, we will guide you through techniques that not only mitigate the intensity of these feelings but also begin the process of reshaping your relationship with them. By the end of this chapter, you will have practiced tools ensuring that you are capable of navigating the turbulent waters of self-doubt with grace and agility, laying a solid foundation for sustained self-confidence.

First Aid Tool #1: Self-Compassion

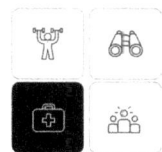

Have you ever reflected on how understanding you are with friends or family members in distress? Imagine a friend upset over a missed promotion, or a child who has scraped a knee. Do you put them down and tell them how incapable they are? Probably not! Chances are, you offer words of comfort. You're likely to empathize and support them through tough times. But when it comes to our own struggles, why is it so difficult to extend the same kindness to ourselves?

In an episode of her podcast *Unlocking Us*, Brené Brown discusses how "people who are mentally tough stay mentally tough because they don't slip easily into shame or self-criticism or self-loathing."[11] This insight opens a new perspective on handling our imperfections – not with harshness but with the same compassion we readily offer others.

Practicing self-compassion is essential for maintaining mental health. It reduces anxiety and stress, increases resilience against setbacks, and fosters a healthier relationship with perfectionism. Self-compassion encourages us to acknowledge mistakes as part of the normal human experience, promoting self-forgiveness and motivating our personal growth. It helps with emotional regulation supporting an overall kinder relationship with ourselves.

Practical steps to cultivate and integrate self-compassion:

1. **Acknowledge Imperfection**: Understand that making mistakes and feeling inadequate at times is a universal human experience. You are not alone in your feelings, and they do not diminish your worth.
2. **Speak Kindly**: Address yourself as you would a dear friend. Shift internal dialogues from criticism to support; change "You can't do anything" to "It's okay to make mistakes."

---

[11] Brené Brown, "Attica Locke and Tembi Locke on Life, Loss, and All Kinds of Love, Part 1 of 2," *Unlocking Us*, November 2, 2022, https://brenebrown.com/podcast/life-loss-and-all-kinds-of-love-part-1-of-2/.

3. **Embrace Your Inner Child**: Sometimes reconnecting with our younger selves helps foster compassion. When you're hard on yourself, offer the kindness you would naturally give to a child.
4. **Reframe Negative Thoughts**: Write down self-judgments and then revise them as you would if speaking to someone you care about. Reading these thoughts makes it easier to recognize their harshness.
5. **Record Words of Encouragement**: Write or record a message of encouragement as you would for a friend. Revisit it when you're feeling down to remind yourself of the compassion you deserve.

By adopting these practices, you not only enhance your ability to cope with personal and professional challenges but also build a foundation for sustained self-confidence. Self-compassion is a skill that, once developed, serves as resource: a mental first-aid kit you can draw on in times of need, turning doubts into a manageable part of your growth.

What?	Being kind, compassionate, and loving to yourself.
Why?	Self-compassion is crucial for emotional well-being.
How?	Develop a self-compassion routine.
When?	Whenever you judge yourself or put yourself down.

My Notes on This Tool:

_____

_____

TOOL	LOW	MEDIUM	HIGH
Impact of this tool for me			
Effort required to implement tool			

First Aid Tool #2: Feelings Matter

While it is astonishing how many intelligent, successful, accomplished, and even famous individuals grapple with feelings of being an impostor – it is also liberating to understand that you are not alone – that many share this experience. It's common for people across all walks of life to feel like impostors at various points in their careers. Acknowledging this can demystify these feelings and make them less daunting. Recognizing you're not alone is vital in managing them.

These feelings while common do not determine who you are: you are not your feelings, feelings are only a temporary sensation. Additionally, it is important not to ignore these feelings but rather to allow yourself to experience them, acknowledge them, and then use methods to manage them effectively:

- **Document Your Feelings:** Begin by writing down what it feels like when these impostor feelings surge. Capturing these feelings in writing helps to process them and see them for what they are: fleeting thoughts that don't define your worth or capabilities.
- **Personal Mantra:** Remind yourself that these feelings are not unique to you. Craft a personal mantra like: "I am not alone, my feelings are not unique, and it's okay to feel this way temporarily." Repeat this mantra whenever doubt creeps in. This helps externalize the feelings as common human experiences, not evidence of personal failure.
- **Personal Reminder:** Develop a visual aid or an audio message that resonates with you, such as a video, a voice recording, a diary entry, or a creatively crafted board. Keep this reminder accessible and turn to it whenever you feel overwhelmed by impostor feelings. Engaging with such a personalized tool can shift your focus and interrupt the cycle of negative thoughts.

When you find that your emotions threaten to overwhelm you, engage with these prepared reflections. Reading or listening to your own insights can interrupt the cycle of self-doubt and refocus your mind on rational thoughts. By consistently practicing this approach, you can begin to dismantle the influence of the impostor feelings and reclaim your confidence.

Acknowledging that your feelings matter and managing how you react to them not only validates your feelings and provides immediate relief but also begins to lay the groundwork for a more confident and assured professional identity. When you implement this consistently, it will equip you to manage these feelings of self-doubt more effectively.

What?	Acknowledge your impostor feelings as common and fleeting.
Why?	It will break the spell the impostor can have on you.
How?	Document your feelings, recite a mantra, and engage with a personal reminder.
When?	Whenever you feel impostor feelings arise.

My Notes on This Tool:

_____

_____

TOOL	LOW	MEDIUM	HIGH
Impact of this tool for me			
Effort required to implement tool			

First Aid Tool #3: Positive Affirmations

Creating and repeating positive affirmations can dramatically alter the story we tell ourselves when grappling with impostor feelings. By embedding these affirmations into your daily routine, you are better prepared to intercept these undermining thoughts when they arise. Positive affirmations act as a mental shield against negative self-perceptions and reinforce a positive self-image.

Positive affirmations help reprogram your thought patterns, reducing the frequency and intensity of self-doubts. They boost your self-esteem and foster a growth mindset by continuously reminding you of your strengths and abilities. This consistent positive reinforcement is key to building lasting self-confidence and resilience. This process taps into the power of self-fulfilling prophecies, where your positive thoughts and expectations can lead to positive outcomes simply because we believe in them and act accordingly.

You can use positive affirmation as daily affirmations or as situational affirmation. For daily affirmations begin your day with affirmations that align with your goals and sense of purpose. Some examples are:

- "I am in charge of my life and every day I am becoming a better version of myself." (taking charge of your life)
- "I will be productive today to work towards my promotion." (furthering your career)
- "I am a skilled negotiator and I will stand my ground." (preparing for an important meeting)

Additionally develop specific statements to counteract situational impostor thoughts:

If you catch yourself thinking, "My colleagues will soon discover that I am not experienced at all" shift to →	"I am grateful to work with skilled colleagues from whom I can learn."
If you're anxious about meeting high expectations after a promotion, reassure yourself with →	"I was chosen for this role because I am capable, and initial uncertainty is natural."

There is a simple way to develop your affirmations. If you have a collection or list of all the compliments, accomplishments, or successes, start there. Extract all strengths, capabilities, and attributes that make you special. Then write positive statements about them such as: "I am competent," or "I am a capable people leader."

Integrate these affirmations into your daily routines – while preparing for work, during exercise, or as part of your meditation practice. Whenever possible do not just recite them in your head but vocalize them to deepen their impact and reinforce your self-confidence, particularly in moments of doubt or stress.

What?	Documenting and reciting positive affirmations – ideally speaking them out loud.
Why?	By repeating the affirmations to yourself, you turn them into deeply ingrained beliefs.
How?	Regularly reciting your affirmations to shift from self-doubt to a robust self-confidence.
When?	Whenever you feel impostor feelings arise.

My Notes on This Tool:

_____

_____

_____

TOOL	LOW	MEDIUM	HIGH
Impact of this tool for me			
Effort required to implement tool			

First Aid Tool #4: Perfectly Imperfect

Are you your own harshest critic? Do you hold yourself to standards so lofty that even when others celebrate your achievements, you feel dissatisfied? It's a common trap: setting the bar impossibly high, aiming for perfection – from your career to your personal spaces. While striving for perfection might seem like a path to happiness and acceptance, it often adds unnecessary stress and anxiety, overshadowing genuine accomplishments and personal growth.

What's the alternative, then? Not pushing harder, but rather accepting that perfection is unattainable and that it's okay to have flaws and make mistakes. Recognizing and accepting our imperfections not only reduces the pressure on ourselves but also enhances our enjoyment of life.

Here are ten practical steps to shift away from perfectionism:

1. **Celebrate Your Strengths:** Take time to recognize and celebrate your achievements. Allow yourself to feel proud.
2. **Embrace Your Uniqueness:** Your individuality is what makes you valuable and lovable. Accepting this can bolster your self-worth.
3. **Relate Through Flaws**: Remember, everyone has flaws; they make us relatable and human.
4. **Set Realistic Standards:** Adjust your expectations to be more attainable and focus on what can realistically be achieved.
5. **Avoid Comparisons:** Comparing yourself to others only fuels dissatisfaction, instead focus on your own journey.
6. **Break Down Tasks:** Tackle overwhelming tasks by dividing them into manageable steps and using checklists.
7. **Make an imperfect plan:** Implement plans that aren't perfect take the pressure off not needing to do it perfectly.
8. **Seek Help:** Don't hesitate to ask for help as you don't have to manage everything alone.
9. **Recalibrate:** Regularly seek feedback and set time limits on tasks to adjust expectations and prevent over-perfectionism.

10. **Monitor Your Progress:** Keep track of your tendencies towards perfectionism and actively work to moderate them.

Letting go of the need to be perfect can be liberating, allowing you to pursue goals that are truly meaningful to you, rather than those you feel pressured to achieve. By embracing your imperfections, you can find fulfillment in the present, enjoying the journey as much as the destination. Create a visual reminder or a memento that you are perfectly imperfect just the way you are.

Embracing imperfection is about understanding that striving for excellence is healthy, but obsessing over perfection is not. Recognize your efforts and the process, not just the outcome. This mindset transforms challenges into opportunities for growth, making every outcome – whether success or setback – a chance to learn.

What?	Accept that you are imperfect and that it is ok!
Why?	You will use less energy and effort on trying to be perfect, letting you focus on things that really matter.
How?	Create a reminder or memento.
When?	At times when you feel that you are not perfect enough.

My Notes on This Tool:

TOOL	LOW	MEDIUM	HIGH
Impact of this tool for me			
Effort required to implement tool			

First Aid Tool #5: Compliments

Receiving compliments can often be much harder than giving them, especially if you struggle with impostor feelings. If you find yourself questioning the sincerity of compliments, suspecting hidden agendas, or fearing that they're merely polite gestures or even mockery, you're not alone. Many struggle to take compliments at face value, interpreting them through a lens of doubt and skepticism. This reluctance to accept praise can stifle self-confidence and reinforce impostor feelings. Learning to embrace compliments genuinely is crucial for building self-assurance and pushing back against those unfounded doubts.

There is an art of receiving compliments. While it might feel unnatural at first, learning to accept compliments graciously is an essential skill for building self-assurance. Here's a simple, effective five-step process to help you embrace praise:

1. **Listen Carefully:** Instead of immediately brushing off the compliment, take a moment to really listen to what's being said. Allow yourself to hear the positive feedback.
2. **Believe in Sincerity:** Assume the compliment is given sincerely. People generally give praise because they mean it, so trust that you truly deserve the recognition.
3. **Express Gratitude:** Respond with a simple "Thank you." Resist the urge to downplay the compliment or redirect the conversation. Accepting a compliment gracefully acknowledges the giver's intent without diminishing your achievements.
4. **Document the Praise:** Keep a record of compliments you receive. Writing them down not only helps in remembering these moments but also serves as tangible evidence of your abilities.
5. **Review Regularly:** Go back to your list of compliments during moments of self-doubt. This can be a powerful reminder of your capabilities and how others perceive your contributions.

Interestingly, the more you practice giving sincere compliments, the easier it becomes to accept them. This practice helps normalize the exchange of positive feedback, making it feel more genuine and less uncomfortable when you're on the receiving end.

By integrating these practices into your daily interactions, you not only enhance your ability to accept compliments but also foster a more positive self-view. Over time, this can diminish the impact of impostor feelings, replacing doubt with a well-deserved sense of accomplishment and worth. Remember, each compliment is a small affirmation of your skills and contributions – embrace them as truths and let them fortify your confidence.

What?	Accept and document compliments.
Why?	Other peoples' opinions about your achievement can help you understand that you are successful.
How?	When someone gives you a compliment, listen and take it in, accepting that it is genuine and sincere.
When?	Revisit the list in times of an impostor hijack.

My Notes on This Tool:

_____

_____

_____

TOOL	LOW	MEDIUM	HIGH
Impact of this tool for me			
Effort required to implement tool			

First Aid Tool #6: Mindfulness

Mindfulness and also mindfulness meditation has emerged as a powerful tool for managing stress, enhancing concentration, and boosting overall mental well-being. Its benefits are supported by a growing body of research, demonstrating that regular mindfulness practice can profoundly impact our brain's neuroplasticity – its ability to reorganize and adapt. Mindfulness Meditation on its own has several benefits:

1. **Enhanced Neuroplasticity:** Regular mindfulness strengthens neural pathways associated with attention and concentration and reduces those linked to stress and rumination. This can lead to better focus and less preoccupation with negative thoughts.
2. **Reduced Reactivity:** By calming the amygdala, the brain's center for emotional processing, mindfulness can diminish the fight-or-flight response, making us less reactive to stress.
3. **Increased Empathy and Compassion:** The practice deepens empathy and compassion, making interactions with others more understanding and less judgmental.
4. **Improved Emotional Regulation:** It helps regulate emotions, leading to enhanced resilience in face of daily stressors.

Mindfulness involves being fully present in the moment, fully engaged with whatever we are doing at the time, without overreacting or being overwhelmed by what's going on around us. This might begin with focusing on a few deep breaths and gradually expanding awareness to thoughts, feelings, and fostering a state of active, open attention on the present by incorporating all five senses, e.g.:

- Going outside for a walk and listening for the sounds of nature
- Feeling the sensation of the soap during handwashing
- Noticing the aroma of your coffee before taking the first sip

These practices help anchor you in the present moment, reducing the impulse to respond to distractions, and improving your ability to focus. They can help disrupt the cycle of self-doubt and anxiety and reset your energy creating a sense of being more grounded. There are many apps – such as Headspace, Calm, Healthy Minds, or Smiling Mind – that teach mindfulness and help track your daily practice.

When impostor feelings arise, mindfulness can be particularly useful. Taking a moment to step back and observe your thoughts and feelings without judgment can help disrupt the cycle of self-doubt. It allows you to handle these moments with perspective, reminding you that thoughts and feelings are temporary and don't define your worth.

By incorporating mindfulness into your routine, you foster mental clarity, emotional stability and create a robust framework to combat the challenges of impostor voices. It's about transforming your inner dialogue from one of doubt and insecurity to one of presence and self-acceptance. Embrace mindfulness as a tool that empowers you to navigate the complexities of life with resilience and poise.

What?	Engage in mindfulness practices to stay present and reduce impostor feelings.
Why?	Reduces your reactivity during impostor moments.
How?	Start to build up a regular practice of mindfulness.
When?	Daily practice and in the moment of self-doubt.

My Notes on This Tool:

_____

_____

TOOL	LOW	MEDIUM	HIGH
Impact of this tool for me			
Effort required to implement tool			

First Aid Tool #7: Have Some Humor

Humor can be a surprising ally within the complex maze of our minds, illuminating the shadows where impostor feelings lurk. Rather than negating our fears, it teaches us to dance with them, turning thought traps into moments of lightness. Consider the exaggerated fears that impostor voices raise: being fired for submitting a report slightly late, labeled incompetent over a typo in a presentation, or worrying that requesting a day off for your wedding could jeopardize a promotion. Will the world halt if you stumble during a speech? Unlikely. Viewing these scenarios through humor's lens exposes the overstated worries of our internal critics, lessening their grip on us. Recognizing the absurdity in these fears lets us laugh, highlighting the disconnect between our anxieties and the reality.

This comedic perspective encourages us to view our fears as exaggerated, improbable outcomes, offering a path from the darkness of self-doubt to the brightness of self-acceptance. Laughing at ourselves relieves pressure and deepens connections with others who recognize their own vulnerabilities in our openness. Humor transforms us from seeming like flawless machines into improvisational artists, gracefully navigating life's dialogues.

Integrating humor into our defense against impostor feelings lights our way, affirming our control over how we respond to these internal narratives. By laughing at the ridiculousness of our fears and embracing our quirks, we reject the notion of attainable perfection. Instead, we rewrite our narratives, portraying ourselves as the protagonists of our own comedic stories, making the weight of impostor feelings as light as laughter.

Embracing humor not only modifies our tactics against self-doubt but also reshapes how we view ourselves, turning the impostor into a humorous companion on our path. The essence of mastering this approach is practice: begin with straightforward, exaggerated examples of your fears, and if you can, involve a friend to counter your doubts with humor. This practice reinforces the age-old wisdom that indeed, laughter is the best medicine, capable of transforming our gloomiest moments of self-criticism into opportunities for growth, connection, and a deeper appreciation of the quirky, imperfect journey of being human.

What?	Using humor to diminish impostor voices.
Why?	Fears and self-doubt are turned into connection and self-acceptance through laughter.
How?	Exaggerate your line of thinking to realize how ridiculous it sounds and laugh about it.
When?	Whenever the impostor voices throw you off your game.

My Notes on This Tool:

_____

_____

_____

_____

_____

_____

TOOL	LOW	MEDIUM	HIGH
Impact of this tool for me			
Effort required to implement tool			

First Aid Tool #8: Embodiment

Embodiment is about much more than just posture; it's a powerful way to influence your emotions and how others perceive you. Imagine someone who enters a room and instantly captures attention without uttering a single word. It's not merely their physical presence, but the confidence they exude through their posture and movements that grabs your notice.

Research has shown that our body language profoundly affects our feelings and behaviors. That there are poses which give us power and those that deplete us of it. [12] This was the conclusion after a decade where a large number of psychologists tried to prove and others who tried to disprove social psychologist Amy Cuddy's concept of "power posing" which had gained a great deal of publicity after her TED talk "Your Body Language May Shape Who You Are". Cuddy suggested that adopting confident postures can significantly boost feelings of self-assurance, even influencing our hormone levels to enhance confidence and reduce stress. These poses alter how others view us–they fundamentally transform our self-perception. By standing tall, with shoulders back and head held high, we genuinely feel more assertive.[13]

Here's how you can incorporate embodiment into your daily routine to combat impostor voices and boost your self-esteem:

- **Choose Your Pose:** Identify a physical stance that represents strength, confidence, or any attribute you aim to embody.
- **Practice Regularly:** Spend a few minutes each day practicing your chosen pose. Morning is a great time to set a positive tone for the day.
- **Feel the Change**: As you hold the pose, focus on the feelings of confidence it evokes. Notice any shifts in your mental state, and embrace the increased self-confidence that comes with it.

---

[12] E, Elkjær et al, "Using Bodily Displays to Facilitating Approach Action Outcomes within the Context of a Personally Relevant Task," *Brain Behavior*, January 2023, 13(1) https://onlinelibrary.wiley.com/doi/10.1002/brb3.2855

[13] Amy Cuddy, "Your Body Language May Shape Who You Are," TED Talk, 2012, https://www.ted.com/talks/amy_cuddy_your_body_language_may_shape_who_you_are.

- **Apply It:** Before entering a situation where you typically feel like an impostor, take a moment for your power pose. Allow the empowerment to fill you, then carry that confidence with you.
- **Reflect on Impact:** After using embodiment in real scenarios, reflect on how it affected your performance and interactions.

Using embodiment during moments of an impostor hijack, can be particularly effective. By adopting a pose that boosts your confidence, you can disrupt the negative spiral of self-doubt. Regularly practicing and applying these techniques helps you gradually integrate confident postures into your daily behaviors. Over time, what begins as a conscious effort to mimic confidence evolves into an authentic part of your self-expression. This process not only helps you appear more confident but also makes you genuinely feel it deep within yourself.

What?	Find a pose that embodies how you would like to think of yourself and how you would like to be seen.
Why?	Body posture plays a significant role in how we feel.
How?	Embodiment works best standing and using your whole body to embody the feelings and goals you want.
When?	In situations when you feel your impostor coming up.

My Notes on This Tool:

_____

_____

TOOL	LOW	MEDIUM	HIGH
Impact of this tool for me			
Effort required to implement tool			

First Aid Tool #9: Get Physical

Physical exercise isn't just about keeping your body fit. It can be a potent antidote to the mental strain caused by impostor feelings. When self-doubt and criticism start to overwhelm your thoughts, physical activity can act as a powerful reset button, offering an immediate release and relief.

This is not new. The link between physical activity and mental well-being has long been well-supported by research. Engaging in physical exercise releases endorphins, the body's natural "feel-good" hormones and this in turn can significantly lift your mood and produce a sensation similar to a natural high. This is particularly beneficial when combating the feelings of stagnation and powerlessness that often accompany a moment of impostor hijack. Getting physically active not only interrupts these challenging mental patterns but also helps you regain control over your emotional state of mind.

When impostor feelings creep up, even simple exercises like a brisk walk, a quick stretch, or a few push-ups can shift your mindset. Activities that demand your full attention – like balancing or sprinting – ensure that your focus shifts completely away from self-doubt, silencing those impostor whispers.

Imagine you're in an important meeting and suddenly, those familiar impostor feelings begin to surface. Rather than sit passively, you could suggest a brief recess and use this moment for some physical activity. Simple exercises like squats, jumping jacks, or a quick dash up and down the stairs could be incredibly revitalizing.

Beyond merely serving as a distraction, physical activities act as symbolic affirmations of taking direct action against self-doubts. They remind you of your own agency and your capacity to alter your current emotional state. This reinforces a powerful sense of self-empowerment and self-efficacy. So, the next time you feel your impostor has hijacked you, remember that moving your body is not just about physical health – it's a strategic move to regain the upper hand and increase your confidence.

What?	Engage in physical activities that require all your attention in the moment.
Why?	Physical activity releases endorphins which make us feel good.
How?	Do whatever is possible in the situation you are in, the more physically challenging the activity is for you the better.
When?	When the impostor voices arise.

My Notes on This Tool:

_____

_____

_____

_____

_____

_____

_____

TOOL	LOW	MEDIUM	HIGH
Impact of this tool for me			
Effort required to implement tool			

First Aid Tool #10: Fact Checking

Fact-checking your impostor feelings is an incredibly effective tool to diminish their influence on your self-perception. When these doubts creep in, it's vital to challenge these thoughts and verify their validity. This critical assessment helps you take a step back and evaluate your feelings against the reality of your abilities and achievements, revealing the often significant gap between perception and fact.

Think of impostor feelings as misleading voices attempting to convince you of something untrue. Just like a deceptive salesperson who will tell you lots of flattery in order to convince you to make the sale. These emotions warp reality, suggesting you're less competent or deserving than you actually are. By applying fact-checking, you separate emotional reactions from actual facts, which fortifies your confidence and empowers you to move forward assuredly.

Think of this process as having a rational conversation with a trusted friend who challenges your self-doubts and points out the lack of evidence behind these feelings. It's about confronting the impostor voices head-on with logical scrutiny.

Here's how you can effectively fact-check your impostor thoughts, using three critical questions:

- **Is there factual evidence to support my feelings?** Look for concrete, undeniable proof that you lack the skills or achievements you feel insecure about.
- **What do trusted colleagues or mentors say?** Reflect on specific feedback from others in your professional circle. Does it support your negative self-view, or does it contradict your doubts?
- **Are there verifiable criticisms or external evaluations that validate my feelings?** Examine any objective criticisms or formal evaluations you've received. Are these in line with your impostor feelings?

Often, you'll find the answers to these questions are an overwhelming "no." This realization helps silence the impostor voices, showing that these doubts are not only exaggerated but also without substantial basis. Recognizing this can significantly change your view of yourself, weakening the grip of the impostor feelings. By regularly practicing this method, you teach yourself to approach these moments with a rational mindset, reducing emotional turmoil and fostering a more confident, fact-based self-image.

Additionally, engaging your network or consulting your accountability buddy to help review these questions can be invaluable. This not only provides external validation but also reinforces your own conclusions with supportive feedback.

What?	Fact check your impostor feelings.
Why?	When we bring in fact checking we realize better how absurdly exaggerated our impostor feelings are.
How?	Have the list with the three questions ready – ideally always accessible such as on your smart phone.
When?	Whenever the impostor feelings flare up.

My Notes on This Tool:

_____

_____

_____

TOOL	LOW	MEDIUM	HIGH
Impact of this tool for me			
Effort required to implement tool			

First Aid: Let's Recap

In this quadrant, we focused on developing a mental first-aid kit to help you quickly intercept and manage the sudden flare-up of impostor feelings. Dedicated to addressing and soothing the immediate emotional turmoil caused by such feelings, this section provided you with a variety of tools designed for compassion, mindfulness, and cognitive reframing. These techniques are not just temporary solutions; they are foundational practices that begin the process of reshaping your relationship with impostor feelings. By integrating these tools, you will enhance your ability to navigate the turbulent waters of self-doubt with grace and agility, establishing a solid foundation for sustained self-assurance and emotional resilience. From practicing self-compassion and embracing imperfection to reframing negative thoughts and reinforcing positive ones, each tool is carefully selected to empower you to handle moments of insecurity effectively and maintain your composure under pressure.

Summary of Tools in the First Aid Quadrant:

1. **Self-Compassion:** Emphasizes treating yourself with the same kindness and understanding you would offer a friend in distress. This tool encourages recognizing your struggles, affirming your worth, and extending patience to yourself during challenging times.
2. **Feelings Matter:** Acknowledges the importance of validating your emotions without allowing them to dictate your actions. This practice helps you recognize that feelings are not facts, and learning to process them constructively is key to resilience.
3. **Positive Affirmations:** Involves reinforcing your self-esteem by regularly practicing positive statements about your abilities and achievements. This helps reshape your internal dialogue to support a more confident and empowered self-image.
4. **Perfectly Imperfect:** Focuses on embracing your flaws and relinquishing the unattainable pursuit of perfection. This approach

encourages acceptance of your human imperfections, fostering a realistic and compassionate self-view.

5. **Compliments:** Teaches the art of accepting praise gracefully, without diminishing its value. This tool helps strengthen your self-esteem by allowing you to truly hear and believe in the positive feedback from others.

6. **Mindfulness:** Utilizes the practice of being fully present and engaged in the moment, without judgment. Mindfulness helps manage stress and anxiety, enhances focus, and improves overall mental health, making it a powerful antidote to impostor feelings.

7. **Have Some Humor:** Encourages finding humor in daily challenges and not taking oneself too seriously. This tool helps lighten your emotional load and adds a refreshing perspective to difficult situations.

8. **Embodiment:** Focuses on aligning your posture and physical presence to reflect confidence and poise. By adopting power poses and other body language strategies, you can enhance your self-assurance and impact on others.

9. **Get Physical:** Recommends physical activity as a way to reduce stress and improve mood. Engaging in exercise can interrupt the cycle of negative thoughts and boost your overall energy levels.

10. **Fact Checking:** Involves critically assessing the validity of your impostor thoughts. This tool helps you challenge and debunk the unfounded beliefs that fuel impostor feelings by encouraging a reality-based assessment of your skills and accomplishments.

By integrating these tools from the First Aid quadrant into your routine, you can effectively intercept and manage impostor feelings, ensuring that you maintain your composure and confidence even under pressure.

Quadrant 2: Cultivate Your Resilience

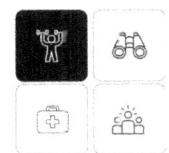

When I met Jenny, she was on the verge of defending her doctoral thesis in the field of engineering and embarking on a postdoctoral assignment. She had ambitions to significantly impact society with her research but struggled with feelings of imbalance in her life. Jenny wrestled with self-doubt, fearing exposure as a fraud, and yearned for increased confidence, reduced stress, and a greater focus on friend-ships, and family. Her ultimate aspiration was to secure a faculty position, lead her own lab and students, secure funding, develop groundbreaking research ideas, and nurture her family.

In her academic environment, Jenny frequently feared expressing herself or asking questions, concerned they might be deemed fool-ish by others. Compounded by the challenge of English not being her native language, she sometimes felt inferior in articulating her thoughts. Uncertain about how to interact with others, she perceived a reluctance from other researchers to engage with her, rendering her academic life in the US dauntingly out of her comfort zone–a situation she was determined to change.

Jenny's reluctance to seek help or collaborate with colleagues underscored the need to bolster her resilience, particularly against procrastination and its ensnaring cycle. With her confidence at a low she engaged her two advisors and several peers to identify areas for improvement and strengths. This unveiled her virtues: a strong sense of responsibility, high standards for her work, excelling in teamwork, and respect of others' time. There was a strong contrast between her own view and the perceptions of her advisors and peers which revealed unanimous praise and recognition of her work surprising Jenny with their positive feedback.

Despite encountering periods when changing her behaviors felt impossible, with certain habits verging on toxic and destructive, Jenny recognized her tenacity and unwillingness to quit. She focused on prior achievements to escape this cycle – mainly focusing on the second quadrant: cultivating resilience. To build resilience, we employed various tools: documenting achievements, learning from failures, journaling, and adopting daily self-care routines including regular meals, exercise, and sleep. Reflections on her progress, peer support, and her unwavering commitment were pivotal in boosting Jenny's confidence, She knew that a healthy routine was essential for enhancing productivity, fostering confidence, and achieving better outcomes. Seeking accountability partners helped ensure adherence to these routines.

Embracing good habits and consistency, Jenny decreased her perfectionist tendencies and started to celebrate daily victories, however small, and shared these with an accountability partner. Despite occasional setbacks, during her appointment as a Postdoctoral Scholar, her perseverance led to publishing two papers in leading academic journals, affirming her sense of belonging in academia for the first time in a while. Her confidence, now bolstered beyond her expectations, influenced her to work smarter, not harder, enhancing her comfort in academia and motivating her to pursue a professorship.

One and a half years into her postdoctoral assignment, Jenny accepted an offer to become an Associate Professor of Engineering at a distinguished US Institute. She now successfully leads her own research lab and her confidence continues to grow. Now as a professor, the impostor voices she confronts are more nuanced, driven by her increasing trust in her expertise, yet she remains vigilant, challenging herself to excel in her field.

The tools in this section focus on the second quadrant of the Impostor Strategy Matrix™. They strengthen emotional resilience to better cope with impostor voices. We'll focus on cultivating resilience by embracing challenges and learning from setbacks. Think of it as the process of tempering steel; through heat and hammering, it becomes stronger and more flexible. We'll explore tools for expanding your comfort zone and leveraging failures as learning opportunities. You'll have a toolkit for building resilience that allows you to bounce back from adversity but approach future challenges with confidence.

Resilience Tool #1: Failures

Yes, you read correctly: failures, plural! Embracing failure is integral to personal growth and transforming those impostor feelings. As we navigate through life's challenges, understanding that failures are not setbacks but pivotal learning opportunities is a game changer. This perspective frees up fears and hesitation and allows us to build resilience.

Imagine you are the end of your life and as you look back on your life you have regrets about what you have not done or where you didn't have the courage to try something new. A fellow coach summed this up "Learning from your mistakes is better than regretting not to have done anything!"

Failure often occurs when we push the boundaries of our comfort zones–whether through innovation, experimentation, or taking on new challenges. It's these moments, though seemingly filled with risk, that offer the richest lessons and most learning – it's where personal development occurs most often. By analyzing our failures, we not only learn what doesn't work but also uncover innovative approaches that might have remained hidden otherwise. Each failure prompts self-reflection, helping us to understand the underlying causes and to better prepare for future challenges.

The growth mindset, a concept popularized by psychologist Carol Dweck, plays a crucial role here. It suggests that our abilities can be developed through dedication, persistence, and learning from failures. This growth mindset is about closing the achievement gap by learning from mistakes.[14] Embracing this mindset means viewing every experience, successful or not, as a chance to learn and adapt.

Henry Ford's notion that "Failure is only the opportunity to begin again more intelligently" captures this approach. Rather than dwelling on what went wrong, we can use our experiences as stepping stones towards, more strategic efforts in the future. This helps transform

---

[14] Carol Dweck, "Carol Dweck Revisits the 'Growth Mindset,'" September 22, 2015, *Ed Week*, https://www.edweek.org/leadership/opinion-carol-dweck-revisits-the-growth-mindset/2015/09.

potential setbacks into possible sucesses, ensuring continuous growth and development.

By reframing how we view failure, we can gain insights from each experience. Instead of dwelling on what went wrong, we can focus on the more strategic efforts in the future. This shift allows us to move forward with confidence, knowing that each attempt, successful or not, generates insights and enhances our ability to succeed in the future.

Thus, by learning to treat failures as opportunities to begin again more intelligently, we empower ourselves to face new challenges with optimism and a readiness to apply the lessons learned. This view not only fosters resilience but also empowers us to approach future challenges with renewed confidence by viewing failures as pivotal learning moments.

What?	Reflect what you have learned from failures.
Why?	When you reflect your failures with the intent to learn, you will not fear to fail again but see it as a learning journey.
How?	Make a list of your failures and what you have learned.
When?	Whenever you have made a mistake.

My Notes on This Tool:

_____

_____

_____

TOOL	LOW	MEDIUM	HIGH
Impact of this tool for me			
Effort required to implement tool			

Resilience Tool #2: Small Wins

Why is it that others can easily recount our successes, yet we often struggle to remember them ourselves? This common phenomenon is deeply intertwined with the brain's wiring and emotional processing, especially when compounded by impostor feelings. Our brains are primed with a negativity bias–an evolutionary trait that makes negative experiences more memorable than positive ones. This bias was crucial for survival but now often skews our perception of our own achievements.

We tend to dismiss our successes, attributing them to external factors rather than our own capabilities. Additionally, the discomfort with self-promotion and the high standards we set for ourselves mean we rarely recognize our achievements as noteworthy. However, overcoming this mindset is crucial for personal and professional growth.

Actively acknowledging and celebrating every success, no matter how small, can shift this skewed perception. Here's how to cultivate it:

1. **Document Achievements**: Maintain a list of all your successes. Regularly updating this list serves as a tangible reminder of your capabilities, especially useful during moments of self-doubt.
2. **Celebrate Often and Early**: Early in any new endeavor, progress can be slow and hard-won. Celebrating these small wins as early victories can help maintain motivation and commitment.
3. **Integrate Celebrations**: Make celebration a standard part of your workflow or personal goals. Planning for these moments helps ensure that you recognize and value your efforts continuously.
4. **Share and Reflect**: Celebrating with others not only amplifies the positive impact of your achievements but also strengthens social bonds and fosters a supportive environment.
5. **Embrace the Journey**: Celebrating each step of your journey maintains motivation and affirms your growth path, gradually shifting your perception from feeling like an impostor to recognizing your true worth.

When we take the time to celebrate our accomplishments, we trigger a cascade of positive neurological responses. The impact of celebrating small wins prompts a release of dopamine, a neurotransmitter associated with feelings of pleasure and satisfaction. This neurochemical boost not only makes us feel good but also reinforces the behavior that led to the success, making it more likely that we will repeat the action in the future.

By systematically acknowledging your achievements and incorporating celebrations into your routine, you reinforce a positive self-image and build resilience against impostor feelings. This practice not only enhances your self-confidence but also solidifies your professional identity, proving that you are capable and deserving of every success you achieve.

What?	Actively celebrate your successes – no matter how small they may seem.
Why?	It becomes real when you celebrate your success.
How?	Document your achievements and and update it regularly. It's more powerful when you share it with others.
When?	Whenever you have accomplished something

My Notes on This Tool:

_____

_____

TOOL	LOW	MEDIUM	HIGH
Impact of this tool for me			
Effort required to implement tool			

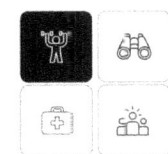

Resilience Tool #3: Social Media Diet

When looking at peers, competitors, or influencers out there it might seem like they have already achieved so much and without any real challenges or setbacks, right? That is most probably wrong! Comparing yourself to others without knowing their entire story can feed your impostor and leads to unwarranted self-doubts. While it is beneficial to challenge yourself, set ambitious targets, and draw inspirations from others, the skewed perception provided on social media is not making us feel empowered. Unless of course you are sharing your own accomplishments or how you have overcome your struggles for others to read.

When scrolling through social media, it's easy to fall into the trap of comparing yourself to others who appear to lead effortlessly successful lives. These polished snapshots can make it seem as if others have achieved great things without facing any challenges or obstacles. More often, it distorts our understanding of success and can amplify our own impostor voices, making us question our own accomplishments and paths even more. It's crucial to remember that social media often shows a curated version of reality, typically devoid of the struggles that accompany success.

Just as any healthy physical diet should be balanced, this is also true for your consumption of social media: consume it with care, balance it, and from time to time leave it out entirely. Engaging with these platforms thoughtfully and selectively is key to maintaining a healthy mental and emotional state. Also which social media you engage in can be helpful. Here are a few tips to consider:

1. **Set Clear Intentions:** Choose social media channels that either help you in your professional life or where your friends are active Limit the number of different platforms you engage in.
2. **Curate Your Feed:** Actively choose to follow accounts that inspire and motivate you, and unfollow those that evoke negative feelings.

3. **Set Boundaries:** Limit your daily social media usage. Not checking social media first thing in the morning or right before bed can also help you feel more empowered.
4. **Social Media Fasts:** Periodically, take breaks from social media for a few days to reconnect more with your own life and goals.

By treating social media as part of a balanced "diet," you ensure that your engagement with it supports rather than undermines your well-being. This helps you appreciate your own journey with all its unique challenges and successes, providing a healthier perspective that fosters genuine self-confidence and empowerment. Remember, it's not about disconnecting entirely but about a healthy equilibrium that keeps your self-esteem intact.

What?	Consume social media diligently, using it only as long as it makes you feel good.
Why?	When you start comparing yourself to others and their polished images, feelings of inferiority can flare up.
How?	Be mindful of your social media diet: how much, when, and for what reasons? From time to time, go offline.
When?	Whenever you realize your impostor feelings flare up!

My Notes on This Tool:

_____

_____

TOOL	LOW	MEDIUM	HIGH
Impact of this tool for me			
Effort required to implement tool			

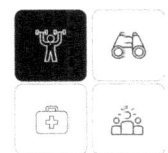

Resilience Tool #4: Mountain of Challenge

Have you ever wondered what makes mountaineers successful who can reach the top of some of the world's highest and most treacherous peaks? Ever wondered what it takes for them to reach those breathtaking summits? Their success often hinges on a mix of crucial factors: physical fitness, technical skills, extensive experience, and deep knowledge of mountaineering. These adventurers are also mentally tough, meticulously prepared, and exceptionally patient. They plan thoroughly, thinking through contingencies and constantly evaluating risks. Their ability to adapt to changing conditions, stamina, endurance, and a profound respect for the unpredictable forces of nature all play a part. In addition, every climb, successful or not, is a learning experience, methodically analyzed to refine strategies for future attempts. Typically, mountaineers start off small, reaching the peaks of smaller mountains before tackling the giants.

The metaphor of climbing mountains also applies for navigating personal and professional challenges. Just as mountaineers don't begin with Mount Everest, your journey to overcoming larger challenges begins with smaller ones. Facing a new challenge might initially trigger impostor feelings, tempting you to step aside and let someone more experienced take the lead. However, each challenge you meet head-on and conquer is a victory to celebrate, increasing your confidence and readiness for more challenging tasks.

With every challenge overcome, you climb higher on your personal mountain of success. What once seemed daunting becomes manageable, transforming fear into familiarity and eventually into confidence. Over time, you'll find that challenges you once shied away from, now invigorate you, and your comfort zone and confidence expand progressively.

As our mind seems to focus on the positive and forgets our struggles in hindsight, documenting these experiences is crucial. Reflecting on past challenges helps you recognize how far you've come, illustrating that your thresholds for stress and complexity have evolved. Just as mountaineers do, you'll adapt your strategies and grow stronger with each ascent. This ongoing process not only prepares you for future hurdles but also solidifies your confidence, proving that you are capable of much more than you initially thought possible. So, start climbing those smaller mountains today, and build the foundation for your summit of success.

What?	View challenges as opportunities for growth and learning rather than threats to your competence.
Why?	With every challenge that you've achieved, you will be more confident of the next one.
How?	Breaking it down bit by bit. Attempting challenges that are a stretch and uncomfortable but still manageable.
When?	When you are at a low define your next mountain, when you are at a high reflect back on previous challenges.

My Notes on This Tool:

_____

_____

_____

_____

TOOL	LOW	MEDIUM	HIGH
Impact of this tool for me			
Effort required to implement tool			

Resilience Tool #5: Stretch Yourself

Eleanor Roosevelt once advised, "Do one thing every day that scares you." This timeless encouragement speaks to the powerful personal growth that comes from stretching yourself beyond the boundaries of comfort. Moving outside your comfort zone is not just about embracing risk—it's about expanding your horizons and discovering new strengths. Why does this matter?

When you commit to doing something that intimidates you or at least feels slightly scary to you each day, you're not just challenging your fears; you're actively rewriting the narrative of what you're capable of. This could be anything from speaking up in a meeting, trying a new hobby, or reaching out to a potential mentor. Each act doesn't need to be monumental; the essence lies in the consistent push against the boundaries you've set for yourself.

This practice of stretching yourself serves multiple purposes. First, it builds resilience. Like a muscle that strengthens with use, your capacity to handle stress and uncertainty grows each time you step into unfamiliar territory. You begin to learn that you can survive discomfort, and this knowledge is incredibly empowering.

Second, it fosters growth. In the zone of discomfort, you are likely to encounter new ideas, skills, and experiences that prompt you to think differently and be more innovative. As you adapt to these situations, you develop flexibility and creativity that enhance your personal and professional life.

Lastly, stepping out of your comfort zone regularly can transform fear into curiosity. Over time, what once seemed daunting becomes an exciting opportunity to learn and grow yet once again. This shift in perspective can profoundly impact your approach to challenges, turning apprehension into positivity, creativity and action.

To truly benefit from this approach, make a habit of reflecting on these experiences. Consider what you've learned, how you've adapted, and how these steps might influence future decisions. This reflection turns fleeting moments of bravery into lasting lessons in courage.

By embracing Eleanor Roosevelt's advice, you not only enrich your life with new experiences but also build a stronger, more adaptable self, ready to take on whatever challenges come next.

What?	Challenge yourself every day to do something that is out of your comfort zone.
Why?	You will gain more confidence by each challenge that you have successfully overcome.
How?	Finding something that is out of your comfort zone and attempting to do it.
When?	Regularly – ideally daily

My Notes on This Tool:

_____

_____

_____

_____

_____

TOOL	LOW	MEDIUM	HIGH
Impact of this tool for me			
Effort required to implement tool			

Resilience Tool #6: Inner Team

Navigating life's challenges often feels like an internal debate, with a chorus of voices each offering their perspective on your decisions. This vibrant, sometimes quarreling gathering of subconscious thoughts plays a crucial role in coping with impostor feelings and building resilience. Friedemann Schulz von Thun's concept of the "Inner Team" provides a compelling framework for understanding and harnessing these voices to enhance emotional resilience.

Imagine your mind as a conference room, where each seat is filled by a different aspect of your personality. Engaging these diverse voices in constructive dialogue can help turn internal chaos into a structured team meeting, allowing you to view problems from various angles and choose the most beneficial team member for the situation at hand.

Here are some ideas you might consider for your inner team:

- The Observer: Silent Witness
- The Critical: Inner Critic
- The Appreciator: Harnessing the Power of Gratitude
- The Wise: Yoda of Wisdom and Resilience
- The Fighter: Beacon of Strength
- The Cheerleader: Motivational Boost
- The Decision Maker: Inner CEO

You can make these dialogues even more vivid and helpful by naming these voices after famous actors, protagonists in books, comic characters, or objects. This inner dynamic mirrors real-world team interactions: with disagreements and alliances. Embracing the diversity of the team – including both motivating and critical voices – is key. Each voice has its role and purpose, and managing this internal dialogue can provide profound insights. By giving the internal voices names and roles, you empower yourself to direct the conversation effectively. For instance, you might call on the Appreciator's positivity in tough situations, or rely on the Wise's counsel to defuse tensions.

Adopting the "Inner Team" not only helps in decision-making and facing challenges but also deepens your self-awareness, highlighting the multifaceted nature of your personality. This awareness equips you to navigate life's by transforming your internal chorus from a source of stress into a council that guides you to grow stronger and more resilient with each challenge.

Moreover, you can harness the full power of your "Inner Team" by adopting the characteristics of one member in particular situations. For example, channel the Fighter's fearlessness during tough negotiations or the Cheerleader's enthusiasm when you need a boost of confidence. Think of it as putting on psychological armor that prepares you for specific challenges and enhances your performance.

What? Engage with the diverse characters of your inner team.

Why? Comprehensive view of your internal perspectives.

How? Identify different personality aspects influencing your thoughts, and engage them in resolving conflicts.

When? Regularly, especially when facing new challenges.

My Notes on This Tool:

TOOL	LOW	MEDIUM	HIGH
Impact of this tool for me			
Effort required to implement tool			

Resilience Tool #7: Gratitude

Practicing gratitude is both an internal acknowledgment and an external expression of appreciation. This transformative exercise deeply impacts our mental health and overall happiness. Rooted in ancient traditions of meditation and mindfulness, expressing gratitude activates neural pathways associated with emotions, social bonding, and well-being.

Every time we take time to recognize and appreciate what we have or where we are in our lives, our brain's reward circuits are ignited, releasing feelings of pleasure and motivation. This isn't just a temporary boost; regular gratitude practice seems to strengthen these neural pathways, making positivity and resilience integral parts of our character. This foundational shift supports the development of a growth mindset, enhancing our ability to recover from setbacks and face challenges with confidence.

In my coaching practice, I've seen firsthand the positive shift that occurs when individuals incorporate even a brief gratitude exercise into their routine. This practice fosters a more compassionate, holistic approach to personal challenges, leaving you feeling grounded and positive, ready to tackle issues with a constructive mindset.

Dr. Laurie Santos, a distinguished psychology professor at Yale University, highlights gratitude as one of the cornerstones of happiness enhancement in her course "Science of Wellbeing."[15] Her research in positive psychology pinpoints practicing gratitude as one of the top ten habits that promote happiness. This act of mindfulness encourages us to pause and reflect on the good in our lives, reinforcing a positive outlook and reducing the impact of negative emotions and stress.

To integrate gratitude into your daily life, consider keeping a gratitude journal. Regularly write down things you're thankful for, or share them with others – perhaps during dinner – as a way to make

---

[15] Laurie Santos, *The Science of Well-Being* (course), Coursera, https://www.coursera.org/learn/the-science-of-well-being/.

gratitude a shared experience. This simple but powerful practice can greatly increase your awareness of life's blessings and, over time, significantly alter your approach to challenges. Cultivating gratitude not only improves your own well-being but also positively influences your interactions and relationships, making it a potent tool for personal and interpersonal growth.

What?	Incorporate a regular practice of gratitude.
Why?	It helps us to be happier, more balanced and resilient and the impostor cannot coincide with the sense of gratitude.
How?	There are various ways to do this such as capturing it in writing, meditating about it in silence, sharing with others or reciting it to yourself out loud.
When?	Daily and when you are hijacked by your impostor.

My Notes on This Tool:

_____

_____

_____

_____

_____

TOOL	LOW	MEDIUM	HIGH
Impact of this tool for me			
Effort required to implement tool			

Resilience Tool #8: Comfortable Getting Uncomfortable

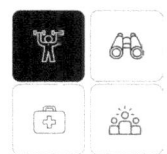

Getting comfortable with being uncomfortable might sound like a paradox, but it's an important skill in today's ever-changing world. It is a mindset which is about more than just enduring discomfort; it's about welcoming it as a catalyst for growth and innovation. When you learn to embrace the unease that comes with new challenges, you unlock a new level of resilience and adaptability that can transform every area of your life. This in turn will create personal and professional growth.

Think of it as mental exercises. Just as athletes push their physical limits to achieve higher performance, you can stretch your mental boundaries to enhance your problem-solving and creativity. Each new challenge, each unfamiliar situation you successfully navigate, continues to build your confidence and hones your ability to handle future challenges.

The first step in becoming comfortable with this kind of discomfort is to recognize the value in these situations. When you're feeling uneasy or hesitant about a challenge, it's often a sign that there is something valuable in your personal development to be discovered. Perhaps you're about to master a new skill, or you're considering a job that feels like a stretch. These moments are opportunities to advance, to innovate, and to evolve.

Starting small and step by step is the basis to foster this mindset. You might start by changing up your daily routine in minor ways, like trying out a new hobby or having something new for lunch. These small changes, while on their own insignificant, build the basis of your tolerance for bigger disruptions. Gradually, what once felt daunting becomes your new normal, and your threshold for what you see as discomforting challenges increases.

However, it is not just about experiencing stepping outside your comfort zone. The real learning and growth come from reflecting on it. More often than not, you'll find that in hindsight the challenge did not seem to be so daunting after all and the outcomes might be really positive. This will help reinforce your new pattern of facing fears head-on and fortify the habit of embracing challenges rather than shying away from them.

By actively seeking out and leaning into uncomfortable situations, you train yourself to thrive in a world where change is the only constant. This approach not only prepares you for the unexpected but also empowers you to seize opportunities that others might avoid out of fear. In the process, getting comfortable with being uncomfortable becomes not just a survival technique, but a strategy for flourishing in complexity and change, and thus uncomfortable situation by uncomfortable situation leaving behind feeling like an impostor.

What?	Embrace challenges which seem uncomfortable.
Why?	By stretching the limits where you feel comfortable you can develop and grow as a person.
How?	By taking on challenges which feel slightly out of your comfort zone.
When?	Regularly.

My Notes on This Tool:

_____

_____

_____

TOOL	LOW	MEDIUM	HIGH
Impact of this tool for me			
Effort required to implement tool			

Resilience Tool #9: Daily Reflections

Reflecting daily is an extraordinarily powerful tool for building resilience and managing the complex feelings that accompany impostor phenomenon. Whether it's during a walk, a meditation session, a conversation, or jotting down your thoughts, you do much more than merely record events – you engage in a reflective practice that fosters self-awareness and emotional clarity.

Think of your daily reflections as a private haven where you can express vulnerabilities without judgment. This practice helps you unload the burden of impostor feelings, dissect them, and begin to understand their triggers. Turning everyday experiences into profound learning opportunities ensures that no lesson, no matter how small, is overlooked.

Imagine starting or ending each day with a quiet moment of reflection – just you and your thoughts. This isn't about harsh self-judgment or dwelling on negatives – quite the opposite – it's a chance to recognize what you have accomplished, learn from what didn't go as planned, and set intentions for the days ahead. Consider asking yourself a few simple questions to guide your reflection: What am I proud of? What do I want to achieve? What can I do better? These questions help you celebrate your achievements and pinpoint areas for improvement.

To see your progress, writing these thoughts down in a journal can be incredibly beneficial – tracking your development over time. Regularly documenting your thoughts about your successes and challenges not only provides a tangible evidence base of your abilities but can also offer immense reassurance on days filled with doubt. Additionally, journaling can be therapeutic, offering a moment to pause and process the day's events or set an intention for the day ahead, serving as a powerful antidote to stress and anxiety. Over time, this practice can help you develop a more grounded and balanced perspective on your professional journey and personal life.

To integrate reflection or journaling into your routine, begin with just a few minutes each day – perhaps in the morning to set the tone for the day or in the evening to unwind. Consistency is key; the more you engage in this practice, the more beneficial it becomes. As you fill pages with your thoughts, fears, and victories, you'll discover that your journal is not just a record of your journey, but a roadmap illustrating how far you've come and guiding you toward future successes.

What?	Reflecting on your daily achievements, lessons, and progress.
Why?	Enhance your awareness of self and your progress.
How?	Reflecting in silence, by speaking about it or writing it down in a journal.
When?	A few minutes daily.

My Notes on This Tool:

_____

_____

_____

_____

_____

TOOL	LOW	MEDIUM	HIGH
Impact of this tool for me			
Effort required to implement tool			

Resilience Tool #10: The Gift

Cultivating a positive mindset is more than just a feel-good mantra; it's a practical strategy to enhance overall well-being and happiness and it is very helpful to cultivate resistance for those impostor feelings. By challenging negative thought patterns and practicing optimism, you can reframe your perspective to see situations in a more positive light, unlocking a host of emotional and psychological benefits.

Shirzad Chamine's concept of Positive Intelligence offers a compelling approach to finding the "gift" in every situation, especially in times of crisis. According to Chamine, every challenging circumstance holds potential gifts and opportunities—we just need the right tools to uncover them. One effective technique I teach my clients is called "The 3 Gifts Technique." [16]

This method encourages you to envision three possible positive outcomes that could arise from any seemingly bad situation, regardless of the timeframe – be it days or years into the future. The worse a situation is or the larger its negative effect, the harder it is to be able to find gifts in this. However, with time and distance, most people find something good to come out even of the most horrid situations.

For the sake of dealing with impostor feelings, we will not look at large scale catastrophes but simple daily matters. For example, consider a project setback at work. The first gift could be the opportunity to demonstrate resilience and problem-solving skills to your management, potentially leading to greater trust and responsibilities. The second gift might involve the team coming together to brainstorm solutions, fostering stronger bonds and a sense of shared purpose. The third gift could be the personal growth you experience by navigating this challenge, which could prepare you for bigger projects ahead.

This technique isn't just about blind optimism; it's about systematically shifting your mindset to recognize and capitalize on opportunities

---

[16] Shirzad Chamine, *Positive Intelligence:Why Only 20% of Teams and Individuals Achieve Their True Potential and How You Can Achieve Yours* (Austin, TX: Greenleaf Book Group,, 2012), 78-79.

for growth and improvement. By regularly practicing this approach, you train your brain to default to a more optimistic and creative state when faced with obstacles, instead of succumbing to despair and negativity.

Adopting this mindset enables you to not only manage but thrive during difficulties, transforming hurdles into valuable lessons. As you continue to apply this approach you'll find that what once seemed like insurmountable problems can become sources of unexpected blessings, teaching you new ways to excel and advance. This shift not only enhances your ability to cope with challenges but also enriches your life, making every experience a stepping stone to greater personal and professional fulfillment.

What?	Looking at the positive in seemingly bad situations.
Why?	It helps shifting our mindset to look for growth and improvement.
How?	Finding the gifts and opportunities in those situations.
When?	Whenever a bad situation happens.

My Notes on This Tool:

_____

_____

_____

TOOL	LOW	MEDIUM	HIGH
Impact of this tool for me			
Effort required to implement tool			

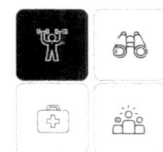

Resilience: Let's Recap

In this quadrant, we focused on cultivating resilience to better manage setbacks and impostor feelings. Dubbed the Modify area, this phase is about transformation similar to tempering steel – through challenges and learning from setbacks, you grow stronger and more adaptable. We delved into tools for expanding your comfort zone, processing feedback systematically, and turning failures into stepping stones. This stage equips you with tools to not only recover from adversities but also to engage future challenges with a reinforced confidence and a robust growth mindset. These practices are designed to solidify your emotional resilience, enabling you to navigate the complexities of personal and professional life with agility and assurance.

Summary of Tools in the Resilience Quadrant:

1. **Failures:** Embrace and learn from failures, viewing them as essential steps towards mastery rather than setbacks.
2. **Small Wins:** Celebrate small accomplishments to build momentum and reinforce positive behaviors.
3. **Social Media Diet:** Reduce exposure to social media to minimize comparisons and focus on personal growth.
4. **Mountain of Challenge:** Visualize challenges as mountains to climb, emphasizing the journey and the lessons learned, not just the summit.
5. **Stretch Yourself:** Regularly push beyond your current capabilities to expand your skills and comfort zone.
6. **Inner Team:** Engage with different facets of your personality to address various challenges and scenarios effectively.
7. **Gratitude:** Cultivate a habit of gratitude to enhance well-being and shift focus from deficiencies to appreciations.
8. **Comfortable Getting Uncomfortable:** Develop comfort with discomfort, seeing it as a signal of growth and learning.

9. **Daily Reflections:** Implement a routine of reflecting on daily experiences to assess progress and adjust strategies.

10. **The Gift:** Looking at any situation which at first sight seems unfortunate and contemplating what the three possible positive outcomes of that situation might be.

By implementing these tools, you fortify your ability to handle pressures and uncertainties with greater poise and persistence. Each tool is designed to strengthen different aspects of resilience, ensuring that you have a well-rounded approach to personal development and emotional fortitude. In this chapter we looked at a comprehensive toolkit to not only survive but thrive in the face of challenges, transforming potential vulnerabilities into strengths, and cultivating your resiliance.

Quadrant 3: Shape Your Vision

Markus, a Senior Business Development Manager in Germany, had advanced his career over the past ten years at a leading global online payments service. Beginning in a support function, Markus swiftly built a reputation across support, operations, and sales. Despite his team's fondness for him, Markus harbored doubts about his leadership abilities, often feeling overshadowed whenever a colleague presented their work or leadership approach. With his peers he avoided speaking on topics where he lacked confidence because he felt like a fraud and that he got his leadership position due to pure luck. He believed he lacked a defined leadership style and training, having pieced together his approach with little guidance. He felt that his self-taught method made it challenging for him to perceive his impact, leading him to feel that his leadership was unstructured and inefficient, and that most of all he needed better time management. Desiring to improve for his team and achieve a better work-life balance, Markus felt drained and his stress levels were high.

Our coaching focused on recognizing his inherent leadership style – characterized by encouragement, motivation, setting vision while empowering his team with ownership and support, and fostering a positive atmosphere – predominately focusing on the third quadrant: shaping your vision. We established clear objectives and key results (OKRs) for his leadership development, prioritizing how he supported and added value for his team. Markus's commitment to these OKRs was evident in his documentation of progress towards achieving his goals.

Markus's commitment to his leadership development and his team's growth began to show remarkable results. His dedication was rewarded when his team received the company's award for Team of the Year, and he was personally nominated as Leader of the Year. This accolade served as a turning point for Markus, allowing him to confront the impostor voices that had plagued him, and affirming his effectiveness and success as a leader. He understood that his vision and goals were crucial in overcoming setbacks, transforming them into opportunities for advocacy and personal growth. A pivotal moment of clarity emerged when Markus received negative feedback on a presentation – a task he was obligated to undertake, albeit with limited freedom to leverage his strengths as he typically would. Instead of being discouraged, this experience underscored the significance of maintaining clear objectives and fostering a strong belief in his capacity to achieve them. This shift in perspective not only fortified his resolve but also highlighted the transformative power of clear vision in leadership.

By the end of our coaching engagement, Markus had not only defined his unique leadership style but also gained confidence in his leadership capabilities, no longer daunted by the prospect of ascending to the next leadership level. He set an ambitious goal for himself, identifying a potential role within the organization where he could maximize his impact by leveraging his strengths—a role that did not yet exist. Markus's journey through coaching led him to plan strategically for achieving this new aspiration, marking a significant milestone in his professional development.

The tools in this chapter focus on the third quadrant of the Impostor Strategy Matrix™. These tools enable you to envision a future where your impostor feelings are part of your success. This chapter guides you through the tools of envisioning your future and leveraging your impostor feelings as catalysts for growth and achievement. We'll explore how to reframe your narrative, setting a course that not only recognizes your accomplishments but also sees impostor feelings as a sign of your ongoing development. By embracing this transformative approach, you'll learn to navigate your journey with a sense of purpose and conviction, turning your impostor feelings from a source of doubt into a superpower that propels you toward your dreams.

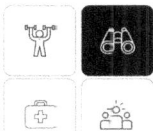

Vision Tool #1: Purpose

Envisioning a future where your impostor feelings become a part of your success story begins with understanding and embracing your purpose. Purpose is the compass that guides your actions, aligns your goals, and gives meaning to your efforts. It's about recognizing that even the doubt instilled by impostor feelings can serve a valuable role in your personal and professional development.

Think of your purpose as your "why" – your life purpose and the driving force behind your aspirations. It's what motivates you to push forward, even when self-doubt and impostor voices whisper that you're not good enough. When you clearly define your purpose, these feelings become less of a roadblock and more of a checkpoint, reminding you to evaluate your path and ensure you are aligned with your true intentions.

Defining your purpose requires reflection and honesty. Ask yourself: What am I passionate about? What impact do I want to have on the world or my immediate environment? How do my unique talents and experiences position me to make that impact? The answers to these questions will help forge a path that feels authentic and inspiring to you. You might also ask your friends and peers to answer these questions about you to get a broader picture.

While your purpose might shift over time, writing it down and having it accessible to you is helpful. You might want to have it visible to you at your usual place of work, or as a phrase in your professional social media for example the tag line in LinkedIn.

Once your purpose is defined, use it to reframe your narrative. Instead of viewing impostor feelings as evidence of your inadequacies, see them as indicators that you are pushing the boundaries of your comfort zone, venturing into areas ripe for growth and achievement. This shift in perspective turns your impostor voices from a source of doubt into a signal that you're on the right track, challenging yourself in ways that lead to meaningful growth.

By embracing this approach, you learn to navigate your journey with conviction. Your purpose becomes the lens through which you view challenges and successes, giving clarity to your decisions and resilience to your spirit. As you align your daily actions with this broader perspective, every step forward, every setback reexamined, and every success celebrated takes on greater significance, propelling you towards realizing your full potential. In this way, your impostor feelings, once a hindrance, become a powerful catalyst for continual self-discovery and achievement.

What?	Having a clearly stated purpose for your life.
Why?	Having a purpose, a clear goal helps us keep the focus on what truly matters.
How?	Brainstorming about your 'why' and then writing it down.
When?	As soon as possible.

My Notes on This Tool:

_____

_____

_____

_____

TOOL	LOW	MEDIUM	HIGH
Impact of this tool for me			
Effort required to implement tool			

Vision Tool #2: Visualization

Positive visualization is a powerful tool similar to mental techniques used by top athletes. Imagine scoring the winning goal or delivering a flawless presentation. This practice does more than just prepare you mentally; it reduces stress associated with performance by fostering a vivid, successful scenario in your mind. Visualization not only enhances performance by focusing the mind and boosting motivation, but it also builds confidence and fosters a positive mindset by emphasizing successful outcomes. Leveraging the brain's capacity to simulate experiences, visualization prepares you psychologically and even physically to perform at your best.

Visualization is not merely daydreaming about success; it involves a detailed and intentional process of imagining how you have successfully achieved your goals. It aligns your actions and behaviors with desired outcomes and thereby setting the stage for real-life success.

Here are five steps to maximize the benefits of visualization:

- **Clarity**: Understand clearly what you want and why. This involves recognizing what you value most and what brings you joy.
- **Details**: Picture the scenario in rich detail, engaging all five senses. The more vivid your vision, the more tangible it becomes, motivating you to making it a reality.
- **Emotions**: Connect emotionally with your envisioned outcomes. Feel the joy, pride, or satisfaction that comes with achieving your goals, enhancing your belief in their attainability.
- **Steps**: Mentally walk through all the steps necessary to reach your goals. Identify and visualize each step, including how you will handle setbacks, as this will help you to be focused on your path to success.
- **Frequency**: Regularly set aside a quiet, undisturbed time for visualization, away from distractions. The best times are right after waking up and just before sleeping.

Regular visualization strengthens the mental image of success, convincing your brain that these imagined scenarios can and will be real. Consistency is key, as it transforms visualization from mere practice to a powerful belief in your capabilities. Tools such as vision boards, placed in visible locations, or written statements of your goals reviewed regularly, can reinforce your daily visualization practice. Some people also find visualization tools or apps helpful for maintaining focus and consistency.

By integrating positive visualization into your routine, you transform your approach to goals. This practice not only prepares you for success but also instills a deeper sense of purpose in your journey, ensuring that your aspirations become an intrinsic part of your daily life and mindset.

What?	Imagine your success including all the possible setbacks and steps you need to take to achieve your goals.
Why?	It prepares you to perform better and achieve your goals.
How?	In a (self-)guided meditative visualization go step by step to what you will need to do to achieve your success.
When?	Regularly, ideally daily.

My Notes on This Tool:

_____

_____

_____

TOOL	LOW	MEDIUM	HIGH
Impact of this tool for me			
Effort required to implement tool			

Vision Tool #3: Vision Board

Creating a vision or a dream board is like mapping out your goals, dreams, and aspirations in vivid color and detail, making them more tangible and achievable. This creative exercise involves assembling images, phrases, and items that represent your aspirations, all laid out on a board to inspire and motivate you every day.

Think of a vision board as a visual echo of your deepest wishes, aspirations and goals. It's not just a collage of random pictures; it's a curated collection that resonates with your personal ambitions and dreams. What does a fulfilled life look like for you? Whether it's images of places you want to visit, reminders of your career goals, symbols of health and wellness, how you want to show up, or quotes that uplift your spirit, each element serves as a daily reminder of where you want to go and who you want to become.

The first step to create a vision board is to make an inventory of everything that you want to be, do or have. Write down all your thoughts, all your dreams without judging or censoring what you think you should write. As a next step look at the list you made and write when you would like to have reached this – in a few months, a year, five years, ten years, etc.?

After you are clear on what you would like to achieve in the future start bringing this to your vision board. Start with a base, like a large piece of cardboard. Gather magazines, photographs, inspirational quotes, and any other materials that you connect with your goals and dreams. As you sift through these items, focus on how each image or word makes you feel. If it sparks joy, excitement, or inspiration, it belongs on your board. It might be an interesting exercise to create your vision board together with your family or with friends, creating a bonding over the joint experience or indeed a joint vision board.

As you place each item, think about what it represents. Is it a new business venture? A lifestyle change? Personal growth? The physical act of arranging these representations not only clarifies your goals but also embeds them deeper into your consciousness. The board represents all aspects of your life. It's a powerful way to visualize your goals and keep you focused on the path forward.

Placing your vision board in a spot where you see it every day – like your office or kitchen – ensures that you have a constant reminder of your goals and the importance it holds for you. This regular exposure helps align your daily actions with your broader life goals, steering your decisions towards realizing those dreams step by step.

The vision board will also need regular updating. As your goals evolve, reflecting on your progress keeps the board alive and relevant. It is a dynamic tool which not only fuels your motivation but also serves as a visual affirmation of your journey, encouraging you to move forward, adapt, and grow. As your visions turn into realities, the board becomes a living testament to your achievements and an ongoing inspiration for future aspirations.

What?	A board with representation of your goals.
Why?	The visual helps to identify more with our goals.
How?	Collage of what you would like your life to look like.
When?	Start now and then update regularly.

My Notes on This Tool:

_____

_____

_____

TOOL	LOW	MEDIUM	HIGH
Impact of this tool for me			
Effort required to implement tool			

Vision Tool #4: Goal Setting

Often the reasons why many of us feel at times like an impostor is that we have raised the bar of what we would like to achieve very high. To navigate this, it's crucial to craft goals that are ambitious yet achievable, designed to bolster confidence rather than trigger overwhelm.

A powerful method to structure goals is the SMART criteria–Specific, Measurable, Achievable, Relevant, and Time-bound. This framework outlines a clear pathway to progress by breaking ambitious visions into manageable steps, which can significantly mitigate feeling overwhelmed.

Specific: Be precise about what you want to achieve. Rather than a general aim like "get better at presentations," pinpoint what 'better" entails – perhaps it means enhancing your engagement with the audience, speaking more fluidly, or reducing your reliance on notes.

Measurable: Set clear parameters to measure your progress and define success. If improving presentations is your goal, measurable metrics might include number of rehearsals, specific evaluations from audiences, or number of times you engage with the audience.

Achievable: Ensure your goal aligns with your current resources, skills, and time. If there are gaps, identify what's needed to bridge them, or adjust your goals to better fit your capabilities.

Relevant: Align your goals with your life purpose and long-term objectives. This connection ensures that each goal isn't just another task, but a meaningful step towards your overarching aspirations.

Time-bound: Set a deadline to add urgency. Whether you're giving yourself a month to polish a presentation or a year to master public speaking, a timeline helps maintain focus and prevent procrastination.

Consider starting with a brainstorming session to clarify what's most important to you. You might want to visualize these in an engaging format, like a vibrant vision board or a detailed spreadsheet, depending on what inspires you and keeps you committed. Discussing goals with someone else can also provide valuable perspectives and enhance your process.

For long-term goals, breaking them down into smaller steps not only makes the larger objective more approachable but also offers regular chances to celebrate small wins. Each minor achievement not only boosts your confidence but also marks your progress, gradually easing those impostor feelings.

By applying the SMART framework to your goals, you systematically validate your efforts and achievements, helping to silence the doubting voices and empowering you to aim higher with confidence and clarity.

What?	Write down your goals and prioritize them, putting a timeframe for you to track.
Why?	The process of goal setting and tracking their progress helps to be focused and set real priorities.
How?	Write down your goals using the SMART framework.
When?	Start now and then track regularly.

My Notes on This Tool:

_____

_____

_____

TOOL	LOW	MEDIUM	HIGH
Impact of this tool for me			
Effort required to implement tool			

Vision Tool #5: Expectations

Setting realistic expectations is an important step for dealing with your impostor feelings. Often, we impose unattainably high standards upon ourselves constantly inviting self-doubt and anxiety. By embracing the concept of achievable, realistic expectations, you can liberate yourself from this self-imposed pressure and take a more compassionate view of your own abilities and performance.

Perfection is an illusion, an unattainable goal that can make every-day tasks daunting and unfulfilling. Acknowledging this can pro-foundly shift your perspective: it allows you to move from striving for the unachievable to progressing through attainable steps. This mindset adjustment reduces the fear of failure by validating that it's normal to encounter obstacles and make mistakes.

Imagine redefining success not as flawlessness, but as continu-ous improvement and learning from each experience. This approach doesn't mean you are settling for mediocrity or not pushing yourself. Instead, it acknowledges the human aspect of growth, which is inher-ently messy and replete with trials and errors.

By setting more realistic expectations, you can alleviate the enor-mous burden of needing to perform perfectly all the time. This view lets you appreciate your own efforts and understand that true growth comes from overcoming challenges, not avoiding them. Every small achievement reinforces your capabilities, boosting your self-esteem and gradually dismantling the impostor feelings.

Moreover, realistic goals create tangible milestones that celebrate your skills and accomplishments. Achieving these goals provides solid evidence of your abilities, further diminishing feelings of inadequacy. Each completed objective is a step towards reinforcing your confi-dence and proving to yourself that you are more than capable.

In summary, adopting realistic expectations transforms your profes-sional and personal development journey. It encourages a balanced, compassionate view of your capabilities and a recognition of your true potential. This not only fosters a positive sense of self but also cultivates a sense of self-worth that is crucial for dealing with impostor feelings. Embrace this transformative approach and watch as it propels you towards genuine, sustainable success, proving that you are competent, capable, and fully deserving of every achievement.

What?	Recognize that perfection is unattainable and set realistic expectations for yourself.
Why?	By achieving incremental attainable goals, you are boosting your confidence.
How?	Setting realistic goals, tangible milestones, and celebrating each completed step.
When?	Start now and then track regularly.

My Notes on This Tool:

_____

_____

_____

_____

_____

TOOL	LOW	MEDIUM	HIGH
Impact of this tool for me			
Effort required to implement tool			

Vision Tool #6: Lifelong Learning

Looking at your professional life as a life-long learning journey can alleviate some of the pressure of having to know it all or be an expert at everything. What if learning is just an ongoing element on your professional journey? Viewing the acquisition of skills and knowledge as a continuous journey with lots of destinations to be visited rather than a final destination enables you to combat feelings of inadequacy and the persistent worry that you're not expert enough or accomplished enough.

Understanding that it's impossible to know everything – and that is totally ok – is a liberating realization. This mindset shift is the first step toward a more sustainable approach to personal and professional growth. Life-long learning doesn't necessarily mean collecting degrees or professional certifications endlessly. Instead, it's about fostering a growth mindset, where every experience – be it a success or a setback – is viewed as a valuable learning opportunity, whereby you will physically grow your brain by actively engaging in learning.

True transformative learning often happens informally, through the rich experiences that come from just doing, simply experimenting, and sometimes failing. It's challenging, if not impossible, to learn from experiences which you have never had because you were too afraid to step outside your comfort zone. Therefore, focus on continuous self-improvement and engage in activities that challenge you and broaden your perspectives.

Once you are committed to life-long learning, you have set the basis for building confidence not only in your current abilities but also in your capacity to learn and adapt, whatever the future may hold. This most likely will take a burden off your shoulders because it is ok, that you do not know everything. It is up to you to decide what skills and knowledge you want to learn. Instead of viewing your skills as fixed and limited, you see them as evolving and quite possibly ever expanding. Expertise isn't about having all the answers – it's about continuously seeking new knowledge and experiences.

Take the time to reflect on what you are learning from each experience – this can be done in meditation, a workshop structure, journaling, with the help of your fan club, mentor, or coach, etc. – and make sure that you document it in a way that is easily accessible to you.

To integrate life-long learning into your daily routine, seek new experiences and embrace challenges. Whether it's through reading a book, attending a workshop, or trying a new task at work, each new experience enhances your skills and boosts your confidence. Make a plan of what you would like to learn – ideally include it in your vision board or goal setting activities and then break them down into manageable steps. This way you have a bitesize journey which reinforces your identity as a capable, resilient professional.

What?	See your life as a continuous opportunity for learning.
Why?	When we see everything as a potential for growth, we are not afraid to make a mistake.
How?	Divide your goal into attainable milestones.
When?	Start making a plan of what you would like to learn now and then track regularly.

My Notes on This Tool:

_____

_____

_____

TOOL	LOW	MEDIUM	HIGH
Impact of this tool for me			
Effort required to implement tool			

Vision Tool #7: Portfolio

Creating a portfolio is an excellent way for visually showcasing your skills, achievements, and the evolution of your learning journey. Unlike a vision board, which visualizes your aspirations, or a success roadmap, which outlines your path to these aspirations, a portfolio displays the tangible outcomes of your efforts and capabilities. It serves as a curated collection of your successes, your accomplishments, and your progress in your professional journey. Even if you are not a visual person, it is much more powerful than simply listing your accomplishments because it does not only demonstrate what you have accomplished but also illustrates your growth and expertise.

In many professions, a portfolio acts as a dynamic résumé presented to prospective clients or employers highlighting past work. However, in the context of transforming your impostor feelings, the purpose of crafting and continuously updating a portfolio goes far beyond mere presentation. It becomes a tool to harness your impostor feelings as catalysts for personal and professional growth showcasing your best work. It's about reminding yourself how you've evolved over time.

Think of your portfolio as your professional diary or storybook. It should narrate your persistence, the challenges you've tackled, the obstacles you've overcome, and the skills you've honed. This isn't merely about putting your best work on display; it's about chronicling your development over time and reminding yourself of the tangible evidence of your capabilities.

To start building a portfolio that truly reflects your journey, begin by defining the narrative you want to convey. Select pieces that illustrate your challenges and triumphs. For example, if you're a consultant, include elements like logos of clients you've worked with, photos from significant meetings or project kick-offs, and any awards or thank-you notes you've received. These items collectively tell the story of your professional impact and growth.

Continually update your portfolio with new projects and skills as they develop. This ensures that your portfolio remains a current and active reflection of your professional life, growing alongside you. Regularly revisiting and revising your portfolio reinforces your self-worth and achievements, serving as a potent antidote to feelings of doubt.

Not only does a well-maintained portfolio boost your confidence by providing concrete proof of your professional evolution, but it also prepares you for job applications, client pitches, and networking opportunities. It transforms abstract skills into concrete achievements, making it an invaluable asset in today's competitive environment.

What?	Create a storybook about your professional journey.
Why?	Showcasing challenges and achievements as a testament of your capabilities.
How?	Collating relevant experiences and graphically illustrate them.
When?	Start now and then update regularly.

My Notes on This Tool:

_____

_____

_____

_____

TOOL	LOW	MEDIUM	HIGH
Impact of this tool for me			
Effort required to implement tool			

Vision Tool #8: Impromptu Actor

Often, when faced with daunting challenges or obstacles, we might initially feel overwhelmed, but afterwards, we realize they weren't as tough as we thought. This transformation – from feeling scared and unsure to embracing, gathering all our courage and inner strength and then feeling accomplished – is like becoming an impromptu actor in our own lives.

Now imagine that you are stepping onto a stage without a script, with an expectant audience before you, and no clear instructions on what to do. This scenario mirrors many real-life situations where we confront tasks that seem too complex, too unfamiliar, or simply too intimidating. Yet, when we bring up the courage to tackle these challenges head-on, we often find that what seemed impossible is actually within our reach, and as a result we grow from the experience.

This approach—acting on the fly and trusting our instincts—goes beyond mere improvisation. It's a vital skill that demands quick thinking, adaptability, and the bravery to step beyond our comfort zones. It's about embracing the unknown with the confidence of a seasoned impromptu actor who trusts in their own ability to adapt and thrive.

When grappling with impostor feelings "fake it till you make it" is like a double-sided sword. However, if you think of being an impromptu actor, it is not about deception, it is about reacting to what is in front of you by using your experience, skills, intuition, and going with the flow. It's about stepping into a role you may not feel fully prepared for and growing into it through experience. You start by acting the part, immersing yourself in the role, trusting in your abilities and just going along without trying to force anything.

For acting "as if" you are totally confident with this role can be a powerful method to build genuine self-assurance. Possibly even taking on the persona of someone confident of whom you are sure that they would wing this situation. By engaging in actions before feeling fully ready, you plunge into new experiences that enhance competence and bolster self-esteem. This isn't about recklessness but recognizing that often, confidence comes after action, not before.

So, the next time you face an overwhelming situation, channel your inner impromptu actor. Take on the challenge, adapt as necessary, and perform to the best of your abilities. With time, the confidence you initially "acted" will start to transform into something real, displacing any lingering impostor feelings with true self-assurance.

What?	Take risks when you do not feel 100% confident by just improvising as you go.
Why?	Your level of confidence will increase with every challenge that you have completed.
How?	Think of challenges that seem slightly too daunting to you and attempt one by one.
When?	Anytime and often.

My Notes on This Tool:

_____

_____

_____

_____

TOOL	LOW	MEDIUM	HIGH
Impact of this tool for me			
Effort required to implement tool			

Vision Tool #9: Opportunities

Embracing and actively seeking opportunities is transformative for your professional development, especially when you often feel like an impostor. Rather than seeing opportunities as random strokes of luck, view them as moments that you can influence with preparation. This perspective shifts the narrative from luck being a serendipitous event to a predictable outcome of your efforts. Roman philosopher Seneca's saying, "Luck is what happens when preparation meets opportunity," underscores this approach. It suggests that your readiness to plan, learn, and adapt is a crucial preparation.

Keith Ferrazzi in *Never Eat Alone* advocates for the importance of relationships in creating these opportunities.[17] He argues that success is not just about what you know but whom you know and how you collaborate with them. This shifts the focus from relying on serendipity to strategically building a network that offers support, advice, and access. Ensure that you are ready when opportunities come your way:

1. **Recognize Opportunities:** Cultivate the habit of being alert to potential openings in your field. This could involve tracking industry trends, staying connected with your network, or simply often being in the right place so that eventually you also will be there at the right time. By keeping your eyes open, you can spot these opportunities early and position yourself to take full advantage.

2. **Prepare Relentlessly:** Preparation is key to seizing opportunities. Develop your skills and expand your knowledge, but also invest time in understanding the needs and challenges of your contacts. This readiness not only positions you to jump at the right opportunities but also to be the first name that comes to mind when your network members find themselves in need of expertise.

3. **Forge Connections:** Ferrazzi emphasizes that networking should not be seen as collecting contacts but as building relationships.

---

[17] Keith Ferrazzi and Tahl Raz, *Never Eat Alone: And Other Secrets to Success, One Relationship at a Time*, (New York: Crown, 2005).

Make your network part of your routine–connect, share, and help. Attend events, participate in forums, engage on professional platforms, and identify influencers. A robust network makes it more likely that you will be thought of when opportunities arise.

4. **Reflect on Successes:** Regular reflection on your successes and how they were influenced by both your actions and your network can provide powerful insights. Understand what worked, what didn't, and how different elements contributed to your outcomes. This helps in replicating wins and adapting your approach.

By focusing on finding and seizing opportunities, you not only counter your impostor but also build a robust framework for professional growth. It reinforces your belief in your own abilities and turns the random nature of opportunities into strategic steps towards success.

What?	Plan and prepare for opportunities strategically.
Why?	Preparation unlocks new opportunities.
How?	Recognize relevant opportunities, prepare for them, build and leverage your network.
When?	Start now and then review update regularly.

My Notes on This Tool:

_____

_____

TOOL	LOW	MEDIUM	HIGH
Impact of this tool for me			
Effort required to implement tool			

Vision Tool #10: Professional Development

Professional development is a cornerstone of professional advance-ment and a critical component of lifelong learning. It's not just about keeping your skills up to date; it's about actively enhancing your abili-ties and expanding your professional network. In today's rapidly evolv-ing job market, more than ever continuous professional development is essential to stay relevant and competitive.

Think of professional development as an investment in your future. Each workshop attended, each conference participated in, and each training program completed not only deepens your expertise but also enhances your standing in your field. These activities are invaluable for not just acquiring new skills but also for networking with peers and industry leaders who can offer new insights and open doors to opportunities.

For example, attending a conference does more than update you on the latest industry trends. It also connects you with like-minded professionals, sparking conversations and potential collaborations. These interactions can be the catalyst for new job opportunities or the start of partnerships that could shape the direction of your career. Such events also offer a platform to be recognized as a knowledgeable professional in your area.

Engaging in professional development builds confidence. Each new skill you master bolsters your self-assurance, essential for tackling daily tasks and embracing new challenges. A pivotal moment in pro-fessional growth is when you transition from learner to teacher. Sharing your knowledge with others not only cements your own understand-ing but also boosts your confidence. Actively scout for opportunities where you can share your expertise your knowledge with others.

Furthermore, consider engaging a coach as part of your professional development path. A coach provides personalized guidance, helping you overcome challenges, leverage your strengths, address blind spots, and actively pursue the life you have always wanted. Coaching pro-vides tailored support and accountability turning potential into action.

Remember, professional development is a continuous journey. It doesn't end with achieving a title or completing a project, but it is a continuous cycle of learning and growth that evolves with your expertise and aspirations. Whether through formal training, networking, or coaching, every step in professional development enriches your skills, expands your network, and strengthens your confidence. Embrace these opportunities and watch how they propel you towards your career goals and transform your professional life.

What?	Strategically select the professional development which supports your growth.
Why?	It expands your skills and knowledge and increases your confidence.
How?	Integrate professional development which enriches your current set of skills, knowledge, and capabilities.
When?	Make it as part of your overall strategic plan of development and growth.

My Notes on This Tool:

_____

_____

_____

TOOL	LOW	MEDIUM	HIGH
Impact of this tool for me			
Effort required to implement tool			

Vision: Let's Recap

In this chapter – the Vision quadrant – we focused on enabling you to envision a future where your impostor feelings become a part of your success. This phase is about actualizing your full potential by aligning your actions with your aspirations. Throughout this chapter, we introduced tools to help you reframe your narrative and leverage your impostor feelings as catalysts for growth and achievement. By adopting this transformative approach, you will learn to navigate your journey with a sense of purpose and conviction, effectively transforming your impostor feelings from a source of doubt into a superpower that drives you toward your dreams.

Summary of Tools in the Vision Quadrant:

1. **Purpose:** Define your core purpose to guide all your actions and decisions, providing a clear direction for your efforts.
2. **Visualization:** Visualize achieving your goals to enhance focus, boost confidence, and reduce performance-related stress.
3. **Vision Board:** Create a visual representation of your goals and aspirations to keep them top of mind and visually inspire your daily actions.
4. **Goal Setting:** Set specific, measurable, achievable, relevant, and time-bound (SMART) goals to pave a clear path toward your aspirations.
5. **Expectations:** Set realistic expectations to maintain motivation and reduce feelings of inadequacy or failure.
6. **Life-Long Learning:** Commit to continuous education and skill development to stay adaptable and knowledgeable, enhancing your professional and personal growth.
7. **Portfolio:** Build a portfolio that showcases your achievements, skills, and learning journey, serving as tangible evidence of your professional development.

8. **Impromptu Actor:** Learn to adapt quickly and confidently in unexpected situations, enhancing your ability to perform under pressure.
9. **Opportunities:** Actively seek and seize opportunities that align with your goals and can propel your career forward.
10. **Professional Development:** Engage in ongoing professional development to enhance your skills, expand your network, and increase your marketability.

By integrating these tools into your personal and professional life, you set the stage for sustained growth and success. Each tool is designed to empower you to not only meet but exceed your aspirations, ensuring that you have the strategies necessary to convert challenges into opportunities and doubts into affirmations of your capabilities.

Quadrant 4: Establish a Support System

Amanda is a biomedical scientist at an American biotechnology company in the US specializing in gene sequencing technology. She played a crucial role as a solo contributor on a groundbreaking project, poised to alter the company's future. For Amanda, contributing significantly and efficiently to a team pioneering breakthrough innovations was crucial, with aspirations to eventually contribute to leadership decisions shaping the company's direction.

She thrived in the execution phase of the business initiative she spearheaded, still in its strategic planning stages. Amanda aimed to manage a small team to bolster this new venture. Despite regularly updating the senior executive team on the initiative and getting great feedback, she battled with confidence issues, yearning for more interaction with senior executives to enhance her confidence and ability to convey complex ideas and thoughts effectively.

Amanda's pivotal challenge was building her self-confidence and executive presence to solicit more feedback, establish credibility, and foster relationships. These steps were vital for amplifying her voice within the company, thereby laying the groundwork for her reputation and the formation of her team. She faced two significant hurdles: the solitary nature of her strategic project work without additional manpower and the denial of support from established departments like communications, business development, or product development.

Our coaching concentrated on boosting her confidence through building up a support network around her – mainly focusing on the fourth quadrant: establishing a support system – incorporating various elements such as leveraging her manager more, getting a mentor, using conferences and networking opportunities to network with like-minded individuals, as well as collecting all the feedback that she has got so far and compiling them into a positive repository.

A check-in with her manager revealed his strong support, encouraging Amanda to seek assistance as needed. He praised her work, particularly her presence and communication within the leadership team, acknowledging her talent and readiness for the challenge. He emphasized the need for Amanda to build momentum and set herself up for success, highlighting the importance of thoughtful content, network building, and industry connections for her initiative's success.

Subsequent sessions underscored Amanda's need for a supportive team to ensure her project's success. In her next check-in with her manager Amanda was surprised to learn of his eagerness for her to expand her network and involve him more in overcoming obstacles. Realizing his genuine support, she strategized her approach to the senior leadership team, aiming to share a comprehensive vision of success, including required resources and support. She devised a system encompassing all internal and external stakeholders, leveraging her network, seeking new networking opportunities, engaging in relevant conferences, seeking mentorship guidance, and using her manager's influence to facilitate discussions with external partners and advocate for their initiative within senior management.

By the end of our coaching engagement, Amanda had successfully enlisted her manager's support and advocacy, advancing external partnerships and conference participation. She emerged more confident, inspired, and capable of steering her initiative towards success.

The tools in this chapter focus on the fourth quadrant of the Impostor Strategy Matrix™. These tools allow you to build yourself a support network of people and resources. This chapter emphasizes the importance of creating a nurturing environment, to maintain and grow your sense of self-worth. From forging meaningful connections with mentors and peers to asking for feedback and advice, we explore how to embed these supports into the fabric of your daily life. As you journey through these pages, you will discover how sustaining a positive mindset becomes a way of life, enabling you to thrive amidst challenges and embrace your impostor feelings as a source of strength.

Support System Tool #1: Role Model

Role models and mentors play an important role in building a support network that empowers you to step outside your comfort zone and manage impostor feelings effectively. They illuminate potential paths through their own experiences of success and resilience, and demonstrate practical strategies for professional and personal growth.

Mentors, in particular, play a dual role. They not only guide and teach but also reflect your current abilities and untapped potential. They help clarify the path to success by sharing their personal stories of overcoming challenges and achieving their goals. They are particularly valuable for those grappling with impostor feelings, as they can provide both examples of success and empathy for the struggles associated with these feelings.

Role models, on the other hand, serve as sources of inspiration and benchmarks for what is achievable. Observing how they handle both their successes and failures can give you inspiration about how to adapt their successful tactics to fit your own circumstances. This helps to foster a mindset that views career trajectories as achievable and normalizes the persistence required to success.

Additionally, consider the concept of reverse-mentoring, where younger or less experienced individuals mentor more seasoned professionals, offering fresh perspectives and new skills. This approach not only enhances learning and adaptation on both sides but also reinforces the idea that expertise and useful insights can come from any level of experience. It challenges traditional hierarchies and can affirm the value of your own knowledge and skills, regardless of your stage in your career. This validation is crucial for shrinking impostor feelings, emphasizes that everyone, regardless of their experience level, has something valuable to offer.

Role models and mentors – both in a traditional and in a reverse relationship – enhance your professional network and provide emotional support that is critical for sustaining confidence and growth. They help you to navigate impostor feelings effectively, turning potential

MAKE FRIENDS WITH YOUR IMPOSTOR!

vulnerabilities into strengths and enabling you to engage with challenges with a more empowered, assured stance.

What?	Find a mentor and role models who you can learn something from.
Why?	Both mentors and role models can help us navigate through impostor feelings.
How?	Mentors can guide us through impostor feelings while role models indirectly serve as our guidance on what or how we would like to achieve.
When?	They are both strategic sources needed to be in place long before we need them.

My Notes on This Tool:

_____

_____

_____

_____

_____

_____

TOOL	LOW	MEDIUM	HIGH
Impact of this tool for me			
Effort required to implement tool			

Support System Tool #2: Feedback and Advice

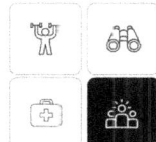

Seeking input from others whom you value, such as a mentor, supe-riors, peers, friends, and a family member or even your competitors or rivals, can be a powerful tool to recalibrate your view of yourself and your accomplishments. Often, we are our harshest critics and we set impossibly high standards for ourselves, fostering a narrative filled with doubts and self-criticism. While you might have your bar raised really high and tell yourself stories of how you might be found out as a fraud if you cannot meet those high standards that you have set for yourself, input from others will paint a more accurate picture of your skills, competencies, and achievements.

However, while feedback is beneficial, asking for advice can often be more constructive. When people give feedback, they tend to focus on past performance, which can lead to vague or judgmental comments. In contrast, advice is usually future-oriented, focusing on actionable steps and opportunities for improvement. This shift from evaluation to guidance helps move the conversation from what was done to what can be done, opening up possibilities for growth and learning.

Seeking advice is a vital tool for recalibrating your self-percep-tion, especially when contending with impostor feelings. While it's common to set impossibly high standards for oneself and fear being exposed as a fraud, advice from others provides a more grounded and realistic view of your abilities and accomplishments. In addition to friendly faces, it can be even more rewarding when asking feedback from competitors or rivals as often their view of us and our successes are much more positive than what we imagine. Getting that reality check and maybe hearing their own impostor voices in the conversa-tion can be informative if not liberating.

Imagine this scenario: you've just completed a project and you're feeling unsure about your performance. Instead of asking a colleague for generic feedback "How did I do?", you ask for specific advice on what you could do differently next time. This not only focuses the conversation on growth and improvement but also helps frame your thinking towards future success rather than past errors.

Regularly incorporating feedback and advice into your routine transforms your approach to professional challenges. It shifts the focus from a fear of being exposed as a fraud to seeing each interaction as an opportunity to learn and develop. By aligning your self-perception with the external evidence of your capabilities and focusing on future growth, you enhance your confidence and motivation. This practice not only diminishes the impact of impostor feelings but also promotes a continuous learning mindset, essential for personal and professional development.

What?	Actively seek feedback and advice from people you value and even those you might dread.
Why?	Often, we tend to believe others more than ourselves.
How?	Depending on your style this could be anything from face-to-face conversations to sending out surveys.
When?	Regularly and when faced with a new challenge.

My Notes on This Tool:

_____

_____

_____

TOOL	LOW	MEDIUM	HIGH
Impact of this tool for me			
Effort required to implement tool			

Support System Tool #3: Fan Club

Having a network of supportive people around you – your very own fan club – can be a game changer when you're wrestling with doubts or feeling low. This group comprises individuals who genuinely care about you and your success, who are there to lift you up when you're feeling down and cheer for you in your triumphs. They're not just spectators; they're active participants in your journey, ready to support you whenever you need it.

Building this fan club starts with transparency and authenticity. It's about letting people see the real you, including those vulnerabilities and insecurities that you might typically keep hidden. Share with them that sometimes you feel like a fraud, that impostor feelings occasionally get the better of you. You'll find that most people can relate to these feelings, as they've likely experienced them too. This shared understanding can foster a deeper connection and ensure that the support you receive is empathetic and tailored to your needs.

Discussing what helps you navigate moments of self-doubt is another crucial step. Whether it's a particular affirmation, a specific type of feedback, or just needing someone to listen, letting your fan club know how they can best support you ensures that they can be effective in their roles. It's not just about them being there; it's about them being there in a way that genuinely helps you.

Encourage an environment of mutual support within your fan club. Just as they support you, offer the same encouragement and backing to them. This reciprocity makes the relationship even more robust and meaningful. Together, you can face challenges more boldly, knowing that there's a safety net of trusted friends and colleagues who have got your back.

In essence, cultivating your fan club isn't just about building a buffer against tough times; it's about enriching your life's journey with meaningful relationships that inspire confidence, foster personal growth, and celebrate every step of your progress.

MAKE FRIENDS WITH YOUR IMPOSTOR!

What?	Surround yourself with a network of supportive friends, family, and mentors who can provide encouragement.
Why?	Encouragement provided by people who matter to you, will help you snap out of impostor feelings faster and can build up your self-esteem and your courage.
How?	Make a list, select and then talk to people who you would like to be in your fan club.
When?	Reach out to selected individuals of your fan club whenever you feel that you are feeling like a fraud or from time to time just as a confidence booster.

My Notes on This Tool:

_____

_____

_____

_____

_____

_____

TOOL	LOW	MEDIUM	HIGH
Impact of this tool for me			
Effort required to implement tool			

Support System Tool #4: Accountability Buddy

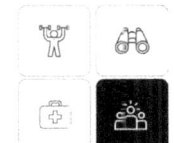

Having an accountability buddy can be a game-changer to achieve any goal but especially when navigating the rough waters of feeling like an impostor. It's like having a personal coach who not only encourages you to stretch beyond your comfort zone but also holds you responsible for the goals you set. This partnership isn't about having a shoulder to cry on – it's about having someone who challenges you and helps you stay on track, especially when impostor feelings threaten to derail your progress.

An accountability buddy is someone you trust deeply, who understands your journey, and who is privy to the fallback plans you've set for moments of doubt. This person is ideally someone whose opinion you respect and who you believe has your best interests at heart. They may not necessarily experience impostor feelings themselves, but they need to understand the impact these feelings can have and be ready to challenge any fallacies you might fall into when doubt takes hold.

This relationship works best when it's reciprocal. Just as your accountability buddy keeps you in check, you do the same for them. This mutual responsibility fosters a deeper commitment to each other's success and ensures that both of you are more likely to follow through on your objectives. The dynamic here isn't just about checking off tasks; it's about pushing each other to grow and pivot when necessary, embracing imperfections along the way.

The role of an accountability buddy is crucial – they act as a mirror that reflects your sometimes distorted self-perceptions and help realign your views with their reality. Their support combines empathy with a necessary dose of tough love, providing both comfort and firm guidance when needed. This can be incredibly valuable, especially when your own tools and strategies seem insufficient to conquer the moment.

An accountability buddy is more than just a friend; they are an essential ally in your ongoing battle against impostor feelings. With their support, you're not just better equipped to manage moments of doubt but also more likely to maintain progress towards your goals. Their presence ensures you never have to face the daunting waves of self-doubt alone, making your journey toward unlocking your hidden superpower a shared and more manageable endeavor.

What?	Find a trusted friend or colleague whom you can confide in, who can serve as a buddy, and with whom you can arrange for a series of measures that will help you.
Why?	An accountability buddy helps us to stick to our plans and achieve our goals.
How?	Confide in that person, explain your feelings, and discuss possible measures and strategies.
When?	Have a first session about this now and then reach out to that person whenever you feel like an impostor.

My Notes on This Tool:

_____

_____

_____

_____

TOOL	LOW	MEDIUM	HIGH
Impact of this tool for me			
Effort required to implement tool			

Support System Tool #5: Superpower Talisman

What successes and achievements can you contribute to how you have overcome your notion of feeling like an impostor? This impostor of yours by your side or at your back constantly challenging you and possibly trying you from becoming your true powerful self. By going the extra mile, working hard, proving to yourself and others what you can do, and ultimately achieving many things that from an outside perspective are very impressive. Each time you have overcome your impostor feelings and have proven that you indeed can do it, you have become more of your true self. It is helpful to have a memento of that – a little reminder of what you really can achieve. Something tangible to help you remind yourself of your true power.

Creating a "superpower talisman" – a tangible reminder of your achievements and resilience against impostor feelings – can be a powerful tool in your personal and professional toolkit. This memento serves as a concrete symbol of the times you've overcome doubts and demonstrated your capabilities, a physical embodiment of your inner strength and potential.

Imagine this talisman as a collection of all the moments you've triumphed over the impostor within. Each milestone or achievement adds a layer to this emblematic totem, from completing challenging projects to receiving accolades or simply mastering new skills that once seemed out of reach. Over time, this talisman grows in significance, each addition a testament to your ability to surpass expectations—both your own and those of others.

What could this talisman look like? Perhaps it's a small, beautifully crafted statue placed on your desk, a custom-made charm that you carry in your pocket, a key ring, or even a framed picture collage of your key achievements. The form matters less than the meaning behind it. This talisman should resonate with you personally, evoking a sense of accomplishment and acting as a visual and tactile counter to any feelings of self-doubt or fraudulence.

Every time you glance at your superpower talisman, let it remind you of your journey: the hard work, the persistence, and the courage you've mustered to prove to yourself and the world that you are capable and competent. It's not just a piece of decoration; it's a beacon of your identity and a celebration of turning your impostor into an ally.

By keeping this reminder in sight or within your reach, you anchor yourself to reality whenever those familiar imposter feelings begin to surface. It tells a story of transformation—one where you continuously convert doubt into confidence and challenges into victories. Let your superpower talisman be a constant, comforting presence that reinforces your true power, whispering a narrative of success and self-efficacy back to you whenever you need it most.

What?	A little tangible object that reminds you of your superpowers. Get creative: it can be anything e.g. charm on a bracelet, symbol on your wallet, sticker on your phone.
Why?	A tangible object that is around you and that you can connect with in a moment of doubt.
How?	The object will have a meaning only to you and will bring you back to your strong, courageous self.
When?	Have it always on you or close by so that you can look at it, or touch it in an impostor moment.

My Notes on This Tool:

_____

_____

TOOL	LOW	MEDIUM	HIGH
Impact of this tool for me			
Effort required to implement tool			

Support System Tool #6: Delegation

Delegation is a powerful strategy not just for managing workload but also for keeping impostor feelings at bay. It can go beyond mere task distribution, serving as a profound affirmation of your abilities and judgment. When you delegate, you essentially recognize and validate your ability to assess tasks and identify who can execute them effectively. This not only boosts your self-confidence but also reinforces your role as a capable leader.

Think about delegation through a slightly different lens–the joy and energy a task brings. While tools like the Eisenhower Matrix help prioritize tasks based on urgency and importance, they overlook an important factor: how much energy the tasks or responsibility provides or drains from you. This is a crucial element as those impostor voices tend to show up less, when we are excited about something and when we are in the flow, truly immersed in the activity, possibly even loosing track of time. Therefore, to enhance your confidence and make delegation effective, consider these factors:

- **Skill Level:** Assess your abilities and skills to perform the task.
- **Energy and Enjoyment:** Reflect on how much you enjoy the task and how much erergy it gives you.

In general, if it's something within your expertise and you enjoy doing it, keep it. On the other hand, if a task drains your energy or you find it tedious, it's a candidate for delegation. By focusing on tasks that you are skilled at and that energize you, you maintain motivation and effectiveness. For tasks that you love but may not excel in, delegate them to someone with the necessary skills, share your passion for the task, and create a learning opportunity for you.

Delegating tasks you don't enjoy frees up energy and allows you to focus on what you excel at, reducing feelings of overwhelm. In addition, watching others succeed in their tasks can be incredibly reaffirming – it not only shows that you made the right call in your delegation but also solidifies your confidence in your decision-making skills.

Delegation Matrix

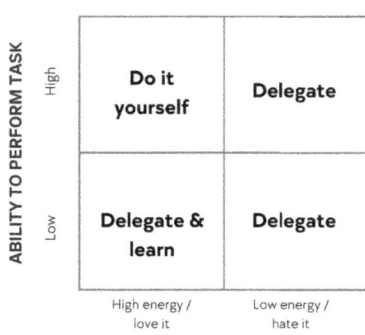

In essence, in order to strengthen your confidence, make delegation be more than clearing your plate, use it strategically as a method to enhance your self-esteem, learn from others, and affirm your capabilities. This makes delegation not just a tool for efficiency but a cornerstone for building up your resilience and self-assurance in your life.

What?	Delegate responsibilities that drain your energy.
Why?	It will free up space and increase your self-confidence.
How?	Delegate using the above matrix where possible.
When?	Whenever you are stressed or need more space.

My Notes on This Tool:

_____

_____

TOOL	LOW	MEDIUM	HIGH
Impact of this tool for me			
Effort required to implement tool			

Support System Tool #7: Networking

Networking is not just a career enhancer; if done strategically, networking can be a powerful tool for mitigating impostor feelings. It alleviates these feelings by providing validation, perspective, and a sense of community. When you connect with others who have faced and conquered similar doubts, their stories and successes offer powerful validation. This reassurance that you are not alone in your struggles is immensely comforting and grounding. Networking serves as a vital means to alleviate impostor feelings in several ways.

Firstly, networking acts as a platform for gaining new insights and affirmations. Connecting with others and hearing how they have navigated similar feelings can demystify and destigmatize your own experiences. It highlights that imposter feelings are common and can be overcome, reinforcing that your doubts do not define your capabilities.

Secondly, networking is vital stepping stone for mentorship and guidance. Establishing relationships with mentors or peers who can offer advice and encouragement boosts your confidence. These connections are invaluable for setting realistic expectations for yourself, developing new skills, and providing a reassuring touchstone when self-doubt inevitably creeps in. Additionally, the feedback and recognition you receive from your network not only affirm your skills and accomplishments but also serve as a counterbalance to any internal narratives that undermine your confidence.

In addition, networking exposes you to a broader spectrum of learning opportunities and the chance to be engaged with individuals with diverse viewpoints. Engaging with individuals from different backgrounds helps expand your network as well as own knowledge and skill set, which in turn will decrease the number and intensity of those impostor moments.

Furthermore, a supportive community is crucial; connecting with individuals who offer understanding and encouragement can create a sense of belonging and shared experiences, diminishing feelings of isolation and self-doubt.

Lastly, being part of a supportive network fosters a sense of belonging, which is essential for quieting those impostor voices. By actively seeking support, feedback, and learning opportunities within your network, you can gradually dismantle the foundations of your impostor moments and emerge more confident in your abilities. Networking, therefore, is not just about building professional connections; it's about constructing a lifeline that anchors you to a community of support, learning, and mutual encouragement.

What?	Expand your professional network for support, learning, and feedback.
Why?	Utilize networking by gaining validation, mentorship, feedback, recognition, learning opportunities, and a supportive community.
How?	Make a strategic plan on how, where, and with whom you would like to network.
When?	Whenever an opportunity presents it.

My Notes on This Tool:

_____

_____

_____

TOOL	LOW	MEDIUM	HIGH
Impact of this tool for me			
Effort required to implement tool			

Support System Tool #8: Broadcast

Breaking the silence about your impostor voices can be a transformative step towards owning, managing, modifying, and transforming them. Often, the shame associated with these feelings keeps many from admitting their struggles, sometimes even to themselves. However, understanding that there's a name for these experiences and that you are not alone can be liberating and sharing your "secret" with others can lift an enormous weight off your shoulders.

One of the most effective ways to break this silence is through enhancing your communication skills, particularly in public settings. Consider enrolling in public speaking classes or workshops. These can not only boost your confidence in expressing yourself but also equip you with the tools to articulate your thoughts and feelings more clearly. As you improve, you'll find that speaking up about your doubts in a structured environment helps normalize these discussions and can also diminish the stigma often attached to feeling like an impostor

On a smaller scale, sharing your vulnerabilities with trusted friends or colleagues can provide significant emotional support. Opening up about your impostor feelings creates a space for honesty and can foster deeper connections with others who might share similar experiences. This act of vulnerability can be empowering, making what once seemed like a personal shortcoming a common, shared human experience.

Additionally, making your goals public to your friends or colleagues can be a powerful motivator. Not only does this create a sense of accountability, but it also builds a community of support around your aspirations. Announcing your objectives around your struggles makes them more real and tangible and it also invites feedback and encouragement, which can reinforce your sense of competence and belonging.

By taking these steps to "broadcast" your impostor feelings and strategies on how to deal with them, you transform your internal

MAKE FRIENDS WITH YOUR IMPOSTOR!

narrative. You move from isolation and silence to community and dialogue, which can significantly reduce the feelings of being a fraud. Engaging openly about your challenges and ambitions allows you to claim ownership of your achievements, your aspirations, and fosters a more supportive and understanding environment around you.

What?	Share your impostor feelings with others.
Why?	It creates accountability, empowerment, and visibility.
How?	Start by sharing it with trusted friends and colleagues.
When?	Once you have set up your individual strategy for dealing with impostor feelings.

My Notes on This Tool:

_____

_____

_____

_____

_____

_____

TOOL	LOW	MEDIUM	HIGH
Impact of this tool for me			
Effort required to implement tool			

Support System Tool #9: Boundaries

Setting boundaries is an essential step for maintaining your mental and emotional well-being, and it is critical for managing your impostor feelings. It's important to recognize that while helping others can be deeply fulfilling and for most of us 'yes' is easier than saying 'no', it only adds to our happiness when we have the bandwidth to do so and when the thing we are saying "yes" to is something that we like and gives us energy (as described in the section about "delegation"). Without proper boundaries, we risk overextending ourselves, which can amplify feelings of inadequacy and fuel those impostor feelings.

One key aspect of setting boundaries is learning to say 'no.' This can be challenging, especially when we fear that turning down requests might be seen as an unwillingness or even inadequacy on our part. However, it's crucial to remember that saying 'no' is not a sign of rudeness or incompetence but a proactive measure to preserve your energy and maintain your quality of work. Additionally, it might be easier to set boundaries without actually having to say 'no' for example: "I can't commit to this right now." or "This doesn't align with my current focus." Establishing these limits helps prevent burnout and keeps self-doubt at bay by ensuring you're not overwhelmed by commitments.

Think of boundaries as your personal security system that guards against the potential overwhelm or triggers for impostor moments. By clearly defining what you can and cannot as well as what you want and do not want to take on, you protect your time, energy, and focus. This clarity empowers you to perform better within your set parameters.

Another vital aspect is to take regular breaks, as they are an integral part of maintaining these boundaries. They allow you to step back, recharge, and gain perspective, reducing the likelihood of stress accumulation and emotional exhaustion. Scheduled downtime is not just a pause—it's an active component of a sustainable work rhythm that supports your mental health and productivity. You are not only setting boundaries on what you do but also on when you are willing to do that and how much of overall time it should occupy.

Ultimately, setting boundaries and giving yourself enough bandwidth aren't just about managing time and resources; they're about nurturing your self-esteem and reinforcing your professional identity. Every time you say a true 'yes' or a respectful 'no,' you are not only managing your resources wisely but also affirming your value and capabilities. By doing so, you will also gain respect and admiration from people around you because you demonstrate that you know your priorities in life and you are willing to follow through on them. By prioritizing your well-being through thoughtful boundary-setting, you create a healthier, more balanced approach to work and life, which is crucial in overcoming impostor feelings and thriving in your endeavors.

What? Define what, how much, and when you are willing to do.
Why?   By defining your boundaries, you can focus on what is truly important to you which increases your self-esteem.
How?   Make a list of your priorities and your boundaries and only say 'yes' if it falls withing your defined bandwidth.
When? Start today.

My Notes on This Tool:

_____

_____

_____

TOOL	LOW	MEDIUM	HIGH
Impact of this tool for me			
Effort required to implement tool			

Support System Tool #10: Professional Support

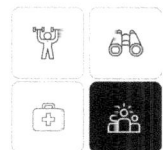

When struggling with impostor feelings – especially if it seems over-whelming – professional support can be an invaluable resource in navigating the complex emotions and challenges. Therapy, counseling or coaching can offer profound benefits in addressing deeper-rooted feelings associated with the impostor phenomena. These professionals provide a safe, confidential space where you can explore your feelings without judgment, helping you to understand and reshape the narra-tives you tell yourself.

Therapists bring tools and techniques from cognitive behavioral therapy and other approaches to help you challenge the distorted per-ceptions that fuel your impostor feelings. For instance, they can help you recognize patterns in your thinking that undermine your confi-dence, such as chronic self-doubt or an overwhelming fear of failure, and teach you strategies to counteract these.

Working with a certified life or leadership coach can also be highly effective. Coaches focus on identifying practical tools and strategies to manage impostor moments rather than delving into their psycholog-ical roots. This can include techniques to boost your resilience, opti-mize your performance in challenging situations, and enhance your self-confidence, empowering you to take control of your professional journey.

These professionals also help build long-term resilience against future moments of the impostor phenomenon. In regular sessions, you can learn to dismantle the automatic negative responses you have towards success and failure with balanced, realistic self-assessments. This process is not just about addressing impostor feelings as they arise but also about preventing them from reoccurring by enabling you to develop a healthier, more confident approach to your achievements and setbacks.

In essence, seeking professional help is a sign of strength and a proactive step towards welbeing and self-care. It equips you with the necessary skills and insights to not only survive but thrive both in your professional and personal life. Whether you're dealing with persistent self-doubt, anxiety, or stress related to impostor phenomenon, a trained professional can guide you towards a healthier mindset and greater self-assurance.

What?	Get professional support for managing your impostor feelings.
Why?	Often we believe external people more than ourselves when it comes to overcoming our self-doubts.
How?	External support can help you objectively mirroring your doubts and feelings of inadequacy.
When?	When you feel this might be beneficial for you.

My Notes on This Tool:

_____

_____

_____

_____

_____

_____

TOOL	LOW	MEDIUM	HIGH
Impact of this tool for me			
Effort required to implement tool			

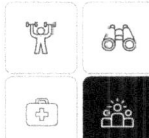

Support System: Let's Recap

In this quadrant, we focused on how to build a support network that aids in developing your courage and extends your comfort zone. These tools help you cultivate habits and create a nurturing environment that reinforces your newfound confidence. We explored tools to establish meaningful connections, and for integrating supportive practices into your daily life. This chapter highlights the importance of deepening your sense of self-worth by building a strong support network around yourself.

Summary of Tools in the Support Quadrant:

1. **Role Model**: Seek inspiration and guidance by identifying role models who embody the qualities you aspire to develop.
2. **Feedback & Advice**: Regularly seek constructive feedback and actionable advice to refine your skills and approach.
3. **Fan Club**: Cultivate a group of supporters who believe in you.
4. **Accountability Buddy**: Partner with someone who helps keep you accountable to your goals, offering mutual support and motivation.
5. **Superpower Talisman**: Use symbolic items like talismans that represent your strengths and achievements to boost confidence.
6. **Delegation**: Learn to delegate tasks effectively to focus on high-value activities that align with your strengths.
7. **Networking**: Expand your professional network to access new opportunities and insights.
8. **Broadcast**: Share your successes, failures, and learnings to establish your expertise and attract further opportunities.
9. **Boundaries**: Set and maintain healthy boundaries for your life.
10. **Professional Support**: Engage with professional services, such as coaches or therapists, to gain deeper insights and structured guidance.

These tools collectively ensure that you have the social and professional backing necessary to face the challenges, turning potential vulnerabilities into avenues for growth and achievement.

PART FIVE

Design Your Own Strategy

Now that you have read and hopefully experimented with all of the tools to provide first aid, to cultivate your resilience, to shape your vision, and to establish a support system when dealing with impostor feelings, it's time to reflect on these tools. We've covered a wide array of tools, each with its unique potential to enhance your professional and personal growth. Now, the challenge and opportunity lie in customizing these tools into an overall strategy to fit your unique journey. This process isn't just about adopting a predefined path; it's about crafting a strategy that resonates with your individual needs, goals, and circumstances.

Assessment of All Tools

To begin crafting your personalized strategy, consider each of the 40 tools we've discussed. Reflect on the following questions for each tool to gauge its relevance and effectiveness for you:

- What speaks to you about this tool? Identify the elements of the tool that resonate most with you. Perhaps it's the structure it provides, the creativity it sparks, or the clarity it brings to a complex issue. Recognizing what attracts you to a tool will help you understand why it might be effective for you.

- What seems daunting? Acknowledge any hesitations or challenges associated with the tool. Understanding these reservations is crucial as it may highlight areas where you need more support or preparation before fully integrating the tool into your strategy.
- What have you experimented with or learned about yourself with this tool? Reflect on any trials you've conducted with the tool. What were the outcomes?
- Did you learn something new about your work style, your stress triggers, or how you handle challenges? Such insights are invaluable as they can guide how you might adapt the tool to better serve your needs.

You might have notice that after every tool, there was a box with two statements:

1. Impact of this tool for me
2. Effort required to implement this tool

With all the information you have now, go back to each tool and evaluate whether its impact is low, medium or high and whether it requires a low, medium, or high effort on your part to implement. By reflecting on each tool with regards to its effectiveness and the effort it requires, you can hone in on the tools that best match your personal style. Consider not only the potential impact of each tool but also how it aligns with your personal sense of joy and flow. The aim is not merely to adopt a range of tools but to adapt them in ways that genuinely enhance your growth and achievement.

If you think of all the tools, in order to derive a perfect strategy for you we can put all the tools into five categories depending on their impact and effort:

- Goblet: Impact high and effort low: those are the ideal tools – a perfect fit for you

Impact & Effort of Tools

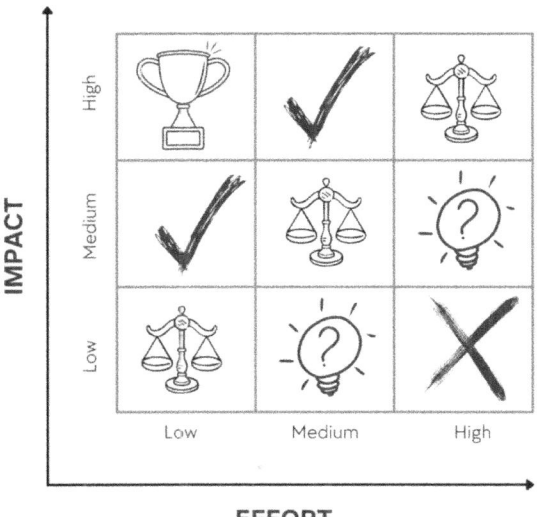

- Check mark: Impact high and effort medium or impact medium and effort low: that is the second-best category with tools that are still relatively great for you
- Balance: Impact high and effort high, impact medium and effort medium, or impact low and effort low: these tools might be worth looking at if you want to expand your strategy in the future or need some alternatives
- Question mark: Impact medium and effort high or impact low and effort medium: these tools might be a stretch for you and at the same time they might challenge you to expand your personal preferences with how you deal with impostor feelings – if you are looking for a challenge those tools might be it for you
- X: Impact low and effort high: these are tools which are not a good personal fit for you – at least at this point in time.

Use the blank Impact and Effort of Tools matrix to transfer all the tools according to your evaluations of their impact and their effort for you.

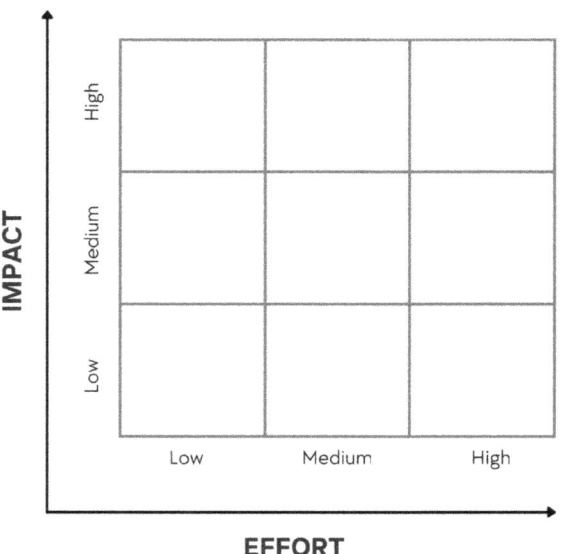

This will give you a good overview of all the tools and how much of a fit or a stretch they are for you at this time.

Selection of Tools

When selecting tools from the toolkit designed to counteract impostor feelings, it's crucial to methodically evaluate their fit based on their impact and the effort required for implementation. Now it is time to creating your version of the My Impostor Strategy Matrix™.

For each quadrant – First Aid, Resilience, Vision, Support – and in the four quadrants below, start transferring all the tools with this structured approach to ensure you craft a balanced and effective personal strategy:

1. **Transfer the Tools**: Evaluate each tool's impact and the effort required for its implementation. Prioritize tools classified as "Goblets," which offer high impact with low effort, making them ideal for achieving significant benefits efficiently and transfer them into "My Impostor Strategy Matrix™."

2. **Balance the Quadrants:** Ensure you select at least three 'Goblet' tools in each quadrant to maintain a well-rounded approach. This balanced selection equips you to handle both immediate challenges and long-term development.
3. **Narrow Down Choices:** If a quadrant has more than three high-impact, low-effort tools, choose those that best align with your current needs and which you believe you'll consistently use.
4. **Address Gaps:** Should any quadrant have fewer than three tools, review those marked with high impact but medium effort or medium impact and medium effort – the "Check Marks". These might require more effort but can be quite effective.
5. **Expand Options:** If there are still gaps, consider incorporating tools which are low impact and low effort, or medium impact and medium effort, or high impact and high effort – the "Balance." While not ideal, they can serve specific needs or supplement your other tools.
6. **Challenge Yourself:** If you're still looking to fill any quadrant, examine the medium impact and high effort or low impact and high effort tools – the "Question Marks." Incorporating these can stretch your capabilities and promote significant personal growth.
7. **Implement and Evaluate:** Put your selected tools into practice and regularly assess their effectiveness. Adapt your strategy based on their performance and any changes in your personal or professional life.

If you should have one or more quadrants where you were done after step 2 – balancing the quadrants – you might want to add a tool to each of those quadrants which will challenge you or stretch you to go out of your comfort zone. The most likely tools for that are tools with a high impact but where your effort to implement them might be medium to high.

This systematic approach to selecting tools ensures that you invest your efforts in the tools most beneficial to you and tailored to your unique challenges and growth potential. By focusing on tools that align

My Impostor Strategy Matrix ™

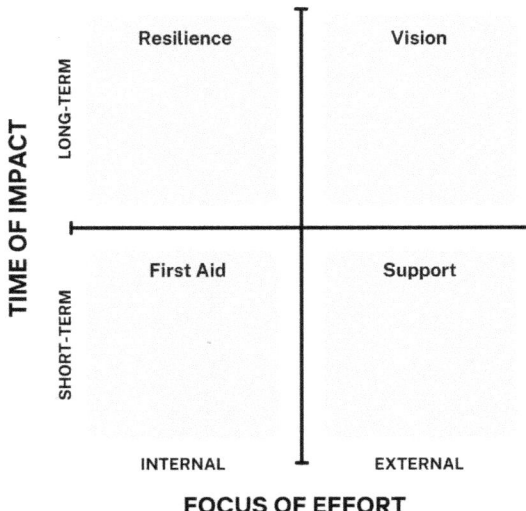

with your goals and managing their implementation wisely, you enhance your ability to navigate impostor feelings with confidence and efficacy.

Now, is this a strategy for life? Probably not. As you develop and grow, you might like to revisit the tools in your Impostor Strategy Matrix™ in regular intervals and check that they still meet your needs, are effective, and you enjoy them. If not, revisit the other tools, assess their effectiveness i.e. impact and effort anew, and select the tools that are appropriate for you at that point in time.

My Commitment

As we close Part Five on deriving your own strategy, it's crucial to solid- ify your commitment to this process. True change comes from consis- tent action, and crafting a personalized plan is just the beginning. To make the most of your Impostor Strategy, you'll need to commit to integrating these tools into your daily life consciously. The commit- ment page is your space to pledge to yourself, ensuring accountability and providing a clear view of your intentions moving forward.

Here's a guide to help you articulate your commitments:

1. **Detail Your Tools**: List the specific tools you've chosen to incorporate into your routine. These should be tools that align with your evaluations of impact versus effort and are tailored to your needs.

2. **Implementation Plan:** Detail how you will incorporate each tool into your daily or weekly routines. For example, if choosing mindfulness as a tool, you might decide to practice meditation each morning before starting your workday.

3. **Set Clear Goals:** Define what you aim to achieve with each tool. These goals should be specific, measurable, actionable, and timely. This could be as specific as improving your public speaking skills or as broad increasing your professional network.

4. **Tracking Progress:** Decide on a method for monitoring your progress with these tools. This could involve keeping a milestone plan, seeking feedback on your progress from peers, or observing changes in your performance and well-being.

5. **Schedule Reviews:** Set dates for when you will review your progress and refine your strategy if necessary. This could be monthly, quarterly, or at another interval that suits your pace of change and the nature of your goals.

Here is an example of how you might summarize your commitments:

Tool	Implementation	Goal	Tracking	Review Date
Daily Journaling	Write in my journal every evening, focusing on the day's challenges and achievements.	To enhance emotional resilience and maintain a high level of self-awareness.	Review journal entries at the end of each week on Friday to identify patterns and adjust behaviors.	Evaluate the effectiveness of journaling on the last day of each month
Accountability buddy	Find 2 people who can serve as my accountability buddies	Helps me be accountable to my goals and offers support and motivation	Check in at least once a month for mutual update	Every 3 months
...	...	...	...	...

This commitment page acts not just as a guide but as a commitment to yourself. It holds you accountable and keeps your goals in focus. By documenting your strategy, you transform abstract intentions into concrete actions, setting the stage for real and meaningful progress in managing your impostor feelings and fostering personal and professional growth.

Notes about my commitment:

_____

_____

_____

_____

_____

_____

_____

_____

_____

_____

_____

_____

_____

_____

PART SIX
What's Next?

As this book draws to a close, let's reflect on what the journey of making friends with your impostor is truly about. Is it about completely eliminating those imposter feelings? Or is it about transforming into someone overconfident or even arrogant? The answer to both questions is: NO! Rather, the goal is to bolster your confidence, enabling you to pursue increasingly ambitious goals without being frequently overshadowed by feeling like a fraud.

While it's likely that impostor voices may never disappear entirely, the intent is to reduce their volume, frequency, and impact. With your personal impostor strategy which you have defined, you can swiftly silence these doubts or, at the very least, manage them effectively without spiraling into negative self-perception. The aim is to cultivate a confident yet humble persona; someone who knows their limits and strengths, and who can step out of their comfort zone with assurance.

This book is not about becoming someone who never experiences self-doubts again – such a person probably does not exist. Instead, it's about evolving into someone who can recognize these feelings for what they are: mere echoes of our fears and not the truth of our capabilities. You're learning to embody the traits of someone who is genuinely humble and confident, who does not see themselves as a fraud but as a continual work in progress, deserving of their successes and capable of learning from their failures.

Remember, overcoming impostor feelings doesn't mean that you will never feel like an impostor again; it means you no longer let those feelings dictate your actions or define your reality.

You are learning to balance humility with confidence, recognizing your achievements without arrogance, and accepting your flaws without self-criticism. This balance is the essence of true growth and enduring self-assurance. As you implement these tools and reshape your thinking, you'll find that what once felt like insurmountable impostor feelings become manageable challenges – steps on your path to genuine self-fulfillment and professional achievement. You will start to make friends with your impostor and unlock it as your new superpower.

APPENDIX
Methods and Tools

The Impostor Phenomenon Scale

Since 1985 when Dr. Pauline Rose Clance has first developec this test, the IP scale has been used as a self-report measure to deter nine whether someone experiences the impostor phenomenon.[18]

The original version can be found: https://paulineroseclance.com/pdf/IPTestandscoring.

---

[18] Clance, The Impostor Phenomenon, 20-22. See also https://paulineroseclance.com/pdf/IPTestandscoring.pdf.

The Impostor Strategy Framework™

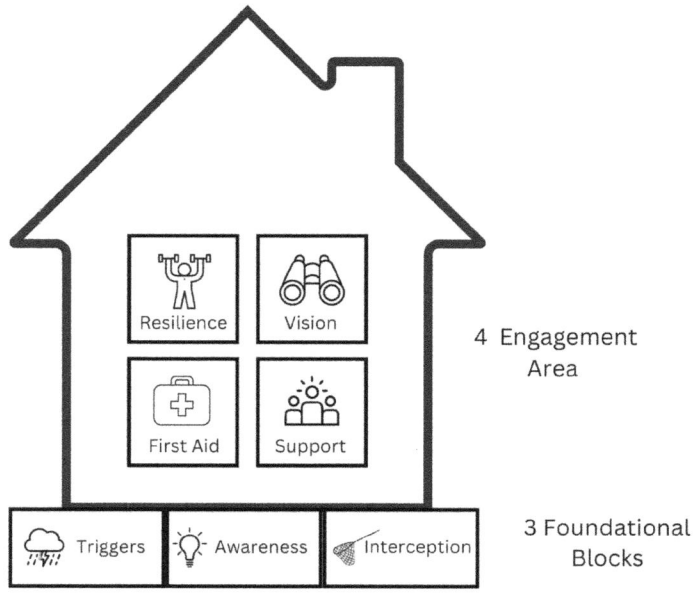

4 Engagement
Area

3 Foundational
Blocks

The Impostor Strategy Matrix™

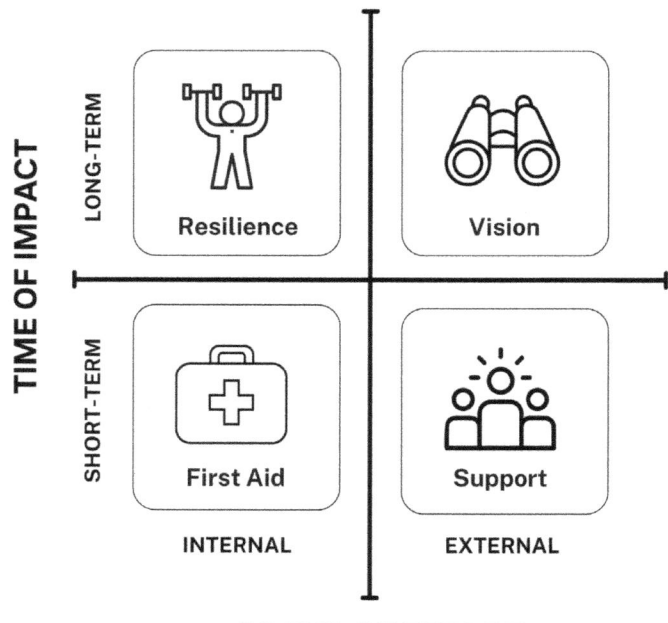

Impact & Effort of Tools

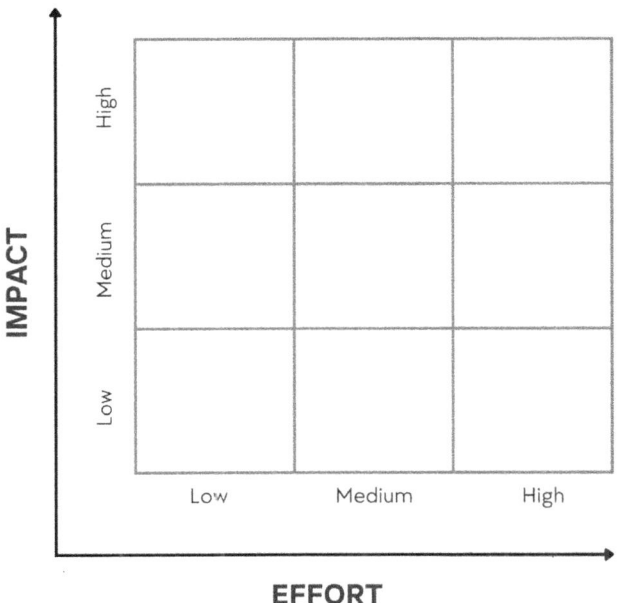

My Impostor Strategy Matrix™

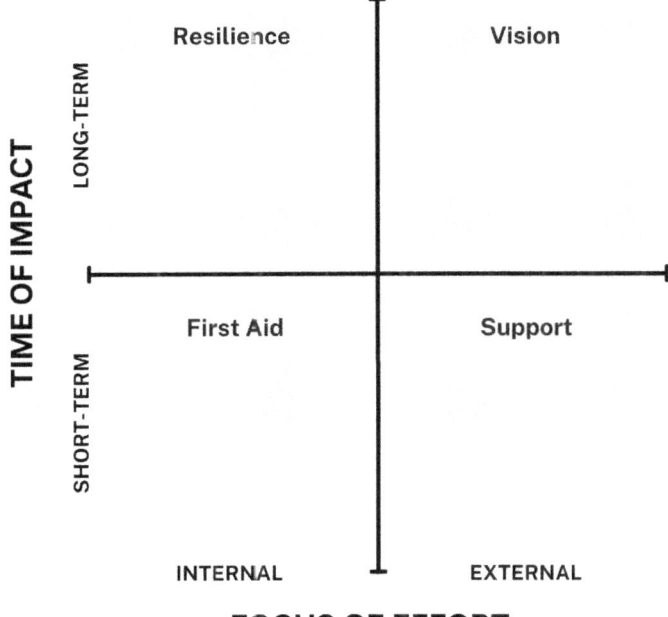

Further Reading

Dr. Pauline Rose Clance, *The Impostor Phenomenon: Overcoming the Fear That Haunts Your Success* (Atlanta, GA: Peachtree Publishers, 1985)

Valerie Young, EdD, *The Secret Thoughts of Successful Women* (New York: Crown Currency, 2011)

Christina Congleton, Britta K. Hölzel, and Sara W. Lazar, Mindfulness Can Literally Change Your Brain, January 8, 2015, *Harvard Business Review*, https://hbr.org/2015/01/mindfulness-can-literally-change-your-brain

Tammi RA Kral, Brianna S Schuyler, et al, Impact of Short- and Long-Term Mindfulness Meditation Training on Amygdala Reactivity to Emotional Stimuli, *Neuroimage*, 2018 Nov 1; 181: 301–313, https://pubmed.ncbi.nlm.nih.gov/29990584

Amy E. Beddoe, Susan O. Murphy, Does Mindfulness Decrease Stress and Foster Empathy Among Nursing Students?, *Journal of Nursing Education*, 2004;43(7):305–312, https://journals.healio.com/doi/10.3928/01484834-20040701-07

Philippe R. Goldin, James J. Gross. (2010), Effects of Mindfulness-Based Stress Reduction (MBSR) on Emotion Regulation in Social Anxiety Disorder, 2010. Emotion, 10(1), 83–91, https://psycnet.apa.org/record/2010-01983-016

B.J. Fogg PhD, *Tiny Habits: The small changes that change everything* (New York: Houghton Miflin Harcourt, 2020)

Tim Blankert, Melvyn R.W. Hamstra, Imagining success: Multiple achievement goals and the effectiveness of imagery. *Basic and*

Applied Social Psychology. 2016 39(1), 60-67 https://www.ncbi.nlm.nih.gov/pmc/articles/PMC5351796/

Anthony Robbins, *Unlimited Power – The New Science of Personal Achievement*, (New York: Free Press, 1986)

Betsy Ng, The Neuroscience of Growth Mindset and Intrinsic Motivation, *Brain Sci.* 2018, 8(2), 20 https://www.mdpi.com/2076-3425/8/2/20

Keith Ferrazzi, *Never Eat Alone*, 2005, p. 42-47

Jaewon Yoon, Hayley Blunden, Ariella Kristal, and Ashley Whillans, Why Asking for Advice Is more Effective Than Asking for Feedback, (Harvard Business Review 2019) https://hbr.org/2019/09/why-asking-for-advice-is-more-effective-than-asking-for-feedback

About the Author

Daphne Dickopf owns a consulting, coaching, and training company and is an ICF-certified executive coach, facilitator, and trainer, specializing in individual, team, and organizational development. Daphne has supported clients globally to unlock their leadership, team performance, and personal growth potential. Her background in international project management and her own leadership experience underpin her belief in every person's innate ability to find the best solutions and chart their path. She holds a bachelor of arts degree in International Marketing from the Regents Business School in London, United Kingdom, and a dual Master of Business Administration from ESSEC Business School in Paris, France, and the Mannheim Business School in Germany. Daphne is also a keynote speaker and an author, with more than 25 years of experience in leadership development.

www.ingramcontent.com/pod-product-compliance
Lightning Source LLC
Chambersburg PA
CBHW051625120626
46551CB00014B/1938

* 9 7 8 1 9 6 1 7 5 7 7 0 7 *

I0624075

Midwest Moonlight

Luna Family Trilogy, Volume 3

Kimberly R. Rose

Published by Kimberly R. Rose, 2023.

To my mom and my grandma - thank you for passing your love for books and reading down to me

Chapter 1

Andrew Luna sighed and lifted the glass to his lips as he watched the newly married couple dance. The church was decorated with plenty of white and flowers, too much of both for his taste. He was happy for his sister. Her new husband seemed to be a good man. But weddings weren't exactly Andrew's scene, they always made him uncomfortable.

"Smile Drew." Lexi, his twin sister, hissed from beside him. "It's their first dance. It's sweet."

Drew gave Lexi an overenthusiastic smile that made her roll her eyes. "Not what I meant," she muttered under her breath.

Lexi wouldn't understand, Drew acknowledged. He glanced at the man sitting beside her in one of the many chairs adorned with a bow on the back. She had found the "love of her life" too, and he wouldn't be surprised if there was a ring on her finger before the end of the year. That was all well and good for his sisters, but it wasn't for him.

"I'm going outside for some fresh air," Drew told Lexi. He slipped past the tables of people celebrating Natala and walked outside. The spring Wisconsin air was cool, and the moonlight lit the grass in front of the church. It felt easier to breathe out here.

"Seems we had the same idea."

Drew turned to see someone had followed him out of the church. She didn't look familiar, but he felt like he'd seen her before. She was shorter than he was, with black hair that seemed as long as her yellow dress.

"Guess so," he replied, walking over to a bench and sitting down.

The woman followed him and sat down next to him, then looked into the sky. "It's so peaceful at night," she commented with a smile that seemed to brighten her face. "I love nighttime. All the kids are asleep, the world is sleeping, and all is calm."

"All the kids are asleep? How many kids do you have?" Drew asked curiously. He didn't know how old she was, but she didn't seem older than him. At only twenty-five, he couldn't imagine having kids right now.

"Oh, gosh." The girl laughed, a blush coming across her cheeks. "I'm sorry. That sounds like I have children of my own." She took a breath to compose herself before continuing.

"I don't have any of my own, but I've been a nanny for four children. Six-year-old twins, a seven-year-old, and the youngest just turned five."

"That's a lot of kids to take care of," Drew replied, somehow glad to hear she didn't have any of her own. He'd also noticed she didn't have a ring on her finger. Not that that meant there was no man in the picture, but it meant she wasn't married. He didn't date married women, that was too complicated.

"They can be a handful for sure, but they can also be a lot of fun. Do you know what one of them asked me before I left? She said, 'Miss Elena, if you are going to a wedding, does that mean you have to have a boyfriend?'" The girl - Elena - laughed again. "It's so interesting to hear how children think. I don't believe she has ever been to a wedding before so she has no idea what that means."

Drew watched her talk, amazed at how bubbly she seemed to be. *Elena was a beautiful name*, he mused. It was a shame she hadn't answered the boyfriend question her charge had asked.

"I'm sorry, I talk a lot. Occupational hazard I think, the children constantly talk and it's a habit I've grown accustomed to. That, and answering endless questions," she beamed at Drew.

Drew chuckled. "I don't mind it," he replied. "I'm a teacher, so I get plenty of questions at my job too. Mostly, 'Do I have to do the homework?'"

Elena's eyes brightened. "You're a teacher? What age do you teach?" She asked enthusiastically. She moved her legs onto the bench, so she was sitting on top of them, facing Drew.

"Sixth, seventh, and eighth grade math." Drew gave her a smile. "So, as you can imagine, I'm a pretty popular teacher. Math being the best subject and all."

Elena giggled. "I always loved math when I was in school. It made sense to me; there was a concrete answer. It was just a puzzle that needed solving. English on the other hand," she sighed. "I always got C's in English. It just didn't make sense to me."

"English is simple enough." Drew shrugged. "I didn't have any subjects that I hated. I guess that interior design elective that I took wasn't my favorite."

"Interior design? That's an interesting choice for an elective. Unless you had dreams of being an interior designer, if that's the case I didn't mean to insult them." Elena's eyes widened in an apology. "It would be a very cool way to be able to tour all kinds of homes or buildings."

Drew chuckled. "No, I definitely did not. I took the class for my sister. It's complicated, she has some health stuff." He glanced up at the moon, wondering how the conversation had gotten personal. Usually, he had a routine when talking to girls, and it included a lot of flirting. He wasn't doing any of that at the moment. Maybe the wedding stuff had scared him out of it.

"So why yellow?" He asked her, staring at her dress. "Most of the people here are wearing pastels or muted colors. You're like a sunflower in a sea of..." Drew trailed off, trying to think of pastel flowers.

"Daisies?" Elena offered with a shrug. "I like bright colors. They are fun and make people smile. Yellow especially is a happy color. Like the sun. When the sun is out, it just makes the day a bit happier. It gives everyone a little something to smile about."

Drew considered that. Elena didn't seem the type of person to be bothered by the extra attention that wearing bright colors could bring. At least that's what he thought upon first meeting her. Most of the girls he dated were the shy, quiet type. He would know, because he dated quite a bit. His sisters, and likely his parents, thought he played the field too much. Sure, he dated a lot of girls, but that's all it was. None of them lasted very long when they learned all Drew wanted to do was take them out to dinner or to do an activity. They were usually looking for something more serious, and serious was something he avoided.

"Andrew?"

Drew turned and saw his mom calling him. He grinned at Elena as he stood up. "Nice to meet you, Elena."

She smiled back at him. "Nice to meet you, Andrew."

He normally went by Drew, but he had to admit hearing his full name come out of her mouth was attractive. *Speaking of which*, Drew gave a quiet sigh when he looked back at his mom and began walking towards her. *Why had she used it? What had he done to make her upset at him today?*

"Andrew, really? Leaving during your sister's first dance? Couldn't you have at least waited until now, when the dance floor is crowded, to disappear?" Connie asked her son as she led him back inside the church.

"I needed some air. I teach in jeans and a nice shirt; these duds are uncomfortable and hot." Drew looked down at the suit he was wearing, glad it wasn't a normal thing. "I wasn't even part of the wedding party. I'm still not sure why the suit was needed."

Connie gave him a warning glance. "Your sister and Tony didn't have a wedding party, for reasons I will never understand." She shook her head. "Regardless, you are family and it is a wedding. Not wearing jeans is a requirement. You asked me to take care of it, so a suit is what you are stuck with."

"I should invest in khakis or something." Drew spotted Lexi across the room, watching the door. She raised her eyebrows when she saw him.

He shrugged and tipped his head towards Connie. Lexi gave a matching shrug, then turned to whisper to her boyfriend. Drew took a breath and watched his mom walk back through the crowd.

The dance floor was crowded now, music blasting through the speakers. Natala and Tony were in the middle of it, doing some sort of line dance from the looks of it. Drew watched his older sister for a moment. He was glad she seemed to be enjoying herself. She likely hadn't even noticed his disappearance.

"You got the lecture from Mom?" Lexi asked as she moved beside him.

Drew looked down and blinked. "I'm family. I must make an appearance the entire time," he replied.

Lexi smiled and followed his gaze. "You could get out there, you know. Dance, enjoy yourself a little bit."

Drew shrugged, glancing at Lexi's wheelchair. Dancing wasn't an option for her, she couldn't be on her feet that long. "Not my cup of tea." He replied, then grimaced. "I don't even know where that expression came from. One of the kids started saying it this week. Long division isn't her cup of tea."

Lexi laughed. "If only that excuse worked, a lot more kids would be using it. They'd only go to the classes they were good at. Maybe Birdie could start teaching candle making, that might be more their cup of tea."

Drew shook his head. Birdie was the science teacher at the middle school, and she also owned a candle making business. A business that employed Lexi as "the detail person". That's what Birdie called her at least. She said that Lexi handled the details. All Birdie had to do was make and ship the candles.

"I'm sure that would be a popular class," he agreed. "But combining children and boiling wax doesn't sound like the smartest idea."

"Not my problem." Lexi frowned, "Or maybe it would be, if the business was involved or got sued or something. You're right, it doesn't need to happen." She glanced towards the front doors of the church. "Do you feel better now that you got that breath of fresh air?"

"So much better. That's why oxygen exists, you know, so people can breathe. Not so they can dance."

Lexi laughed. "Come sit down then, talk to Cameron and me. I'm trying to convince him to add a raised gardening bed to his backyard."

"Do you know anything about gardening?" Drew asked. It wasn't hard to get through a crowd when you were following the girl in the wheelchair. "Is this another thing I'm going to be roped into helping with?"

Cameron - Lexi's boyfriend - was his neighbor. Because of this, he'd been dragged into a couple backyard projects, as in Lexi's words - "he was there". Although, for all the times one of his foster dogs had made it into Cameron's backyard, he supposed he owed the guy something.

As Drew settled back into his chair and tried to pay attention to the conversation Cameron and Lexi were having about the gardening beds, his attention was drawn to the doorway. Elena strolled back into the church, her dress swishing as she walked. His attention was drawn to her legs, which somehow looked perfectly smooth and tanned.

"Drew?" Lexi asked, snapping her fingers in front of his face. "I've been talking to you for at least thirty seconds, and you haven't been paying any attention."

"Sorry." Drew muttered, not really sorry at all. He pulled his gaze away from Elena as he looked at his sister. "What do you want?"

"What makes you think I want something?" Lexi asked with a fake pout.

Cameron chuckled and put his hand on Lexi's shoulder. "He knows you too well."

Lexi sighed, ignoring her boyfriend. "The garden beds. Do you think you could build them?" She gave him the wide-eyed look that always made him feel like he needed to help her. "Cameron is working twelves for the next three days, and I really want to get planting."

"Lexi, it's April." Drew looked out the window of the church, where the grass was miraculously showing and somehow green. "We could get a snowstorm next week. It's way too early to be planting anything outdoors."

"Nope, don't wish that into existence." Lexi covered her ears as if that would make Drew's words go away. "I don't want to hear it; I don't even want to think about it. There's been enough snow, we are done and its summer now."

"It's most definitely not summer," Drew commented, thinking about the cool air he'd felt. "Spring, maybe. But in Wisconsin, snow in spring isn't uncommon."

Lexi's shoulders fell. She glared at her brother as she picked up her glass. "You're no help," she accused, before taking a sip of her water.

Drew picked up his own glass and raised it as if he was going to toast. "That's what I'm here for," he replied. He looked around the room, wondering where Elena had gone. There was something about her that interested him.

Lexi watched him, then scanned the room. She widened her eyes when she spotted Elena. "Andrew Luna." she hissed in a shocked whisper. "Don't even think about it. Seriously, she can't be one of your girls."

Drew frowned. It wasn't like Lexi to warn him away from anyone. She was usually one to sit back and watch as she rolled her eyes.

"Why not?" He asked, his eyes following Elena as she walked over to Natala and Tony. "She's cute. And she followed me outside, I talked to her for a couple minutes. She's a nanny. We both work with kids. Already have plenty in common."

Lexi narrowed her eyes as she watched Elena hug Tony, then Natala. "Because, idiot, she's Tony's little sister."

Drew watched her and Tony speak, trying to see if there were any similarities. They didn't look that much alike; he wouldn't have pegged them for siblings. Then again, he and Lexi didn't look much alike either, and they were twins. "We will see," he replied casually.

Lexi shot a worried glance at Cameron, who shrugged. "I'm an only child. I have no advice for anyone in this situation."

"Sometimes I wish I was an only child." Lexi took another sip of her water as she watched Drew, who seemed oblivious to her. "I do not want to be caught in the middle of anything."

Natala walked away from Elena and Tony to join her siblings at their table. "Where are Mom and Dad?" She asked as she removed the high heels she was wearing.

Drew watched her rub her feet. "I'm not sure, but they better be here. Mom already yelled at me once for going outside to breathe."

Natala giggled. "I would have thought it would be Lexi that had trouble breathing, not you."

Lexi had a chronic illness that affected her atomic nervous system. Sometimes that caused breathing to be more difficult for her than it would be for the average person.

"Not funny Natala." Lexi shook her head, unable to keep the smile off her face. "Why do you wear those heels if they hurt your feet so much?"

Natala shrugged, kicking them under the table. "They are pretty, and I like them. Shoes aren't for comfort."

Drew looked down at the tennis shoes he'd worn with his suit, surprised and pleased they'd escaped his mother's notice. "They should be. Ask anyone at school. I think we all wear shoes more for comfort than style. Teachers, at least. The kids have a different opinion."

Natala playfully swatted his arm. "At work, yes. You think I wear heels all day to the factory? Not a chance. But this is my wedding, and I wanted to wear pretty shoes."

"As much as I enjoy talking about shoes, I think I'm going to head out. I've got to be at the hospital in a couple of hours." Cameron kissed Lexi, then stood up. "Drew, nice to see you man. Congrats Natala, it was a beautiful wedding."

Natala stood to give him a hug. "Thank you for coming," she replied. Drew glanced at Lexi. "Are you heading out too?" He asked her.

"Nope, I'm going to stick it out with you." She smirked. "I like seeing you uncomfortable. It's a new look. I think you should go to formal events more often."

"Who wants to go to formal events more often? I'd rather be in the classroom any day."

Chapter 2

The next morning, Drew got up and quickly took a shower. He and the rest of the family were having brunch so Natala and Tony could open their wedding gifts. Something that was apparently normal.

He'd never been close to anyone getting married before, so if it was a normal thing he wouldn't know. As Drew made a quick protein drink, he glanced over at Cameron's house. All the lights were out. He must be at the hospital.

Drew was a little jealous that Cameron had gotten out of the brunch. Teachers didn't often work Saturdays, so he couldn't use word for an excuse. Or if there were papers to grade or something like that, it could usually be done at any point on the weekend.

His phone buzzed right before he turned on the blender. With one hand on the blender to keep the lid on, Drew unlocked his phone with the other hand. He sighed when he saw the text had come from Lexi.

Are you going to be here soon? Daisy and I are feeling lonely, Mom and Dad are reminiscing about their own wedding. Not that it's bad but I can only take so much of this.

Drew chuckled. *That's why I moved out, to avoid all the weird conversations. I'm walking over in a sec.* He sent that text, then stopped the blender. Grabbing a cup that may or may not have been washed yet, he dumped the protein drink into it and screwed the lid on.

"Do I need to take anything?" He asked aloud, scanning the house. He dropped his keys into his pocket along with his phone, then shrugged and left the house.

Brunch was being held at his parents'. As they only lived a couple blocks away it seemed easiest to just walk over there. And it was perfect weather for a walk, nice and cool but not freezing.

It only took Drew five minutes to walk over to the house. He let himself inside when he got there. "Lexi?" He called as he walked into the kitchen.

"Outside!" Lexi called through the screen door. Drew opened the sliding door and stepped outside, surprised to find their porch now held a large table and chairs. "Where did this come from?" He asked as he sat down in one of the chairs.

"A very nice rental place. They delivered it yesterday and they will pick it back up today. I thought it would be perfect for brunch," Connie told him as she walked past. "There will be enough people that the normal dining table will be crowded. It's finally warm enough to spend some time out here."

Drew looked over at Lexi, who shrugged. "Don't ask me," she mouthed, her eyes moving to the grass where David was setting up the cornhole game.

"Drew, would you go get the door?" Connie asked him as she walked past, a bowl full of muffins in hand. "I just heard the doorbell ring."

"Sure." Drew replied, glad he could be of assistance somehow. He made his way through the house to the front door, and opened it. It surprised him to see Elena standing there. *Tony's sister,* he remembered. *If I'm stuck being at this thing, it makes sense she would be here as well.*

"Hello again," he greeted her with a smile, opening the door.

"Andrew?" Elena smiled. "I wasn't expecting to see you here. Are you related to Natala? Maybe I should have asked you that yesterday, but it slipped my mind with all the people. They all knew someone in some capacity, but that didn't tell me how close anyone was."

Drew tried to hide his amusement as he led Elena through the house to the backyard. She seemed to use more words than anyone else he knew when speaking. For some reason it was attractive. "Natala is my sister."

Elena's eyes widened, and she froze. "You're one of the twins?" She asked, studying him. "Natala told me she had younger siblings that were twins. I bet you and your sister were a handful for your mother growing up." She shuddered. "Twins are a different breed, not that I mean any offense. I just find it fascinating the connection they have."

Drew remembered she'd said yesterday that two of her charges were twins. She must have her hands full. "You'd have to ask my mother that. I don't remember how much of a problem I was." He smirked at her. "And if I did, I probably wouldn't admit that."

Elena laughed. "That sounds plenty accurate," she replied. Drew opened the screen door for her to walk outside, then followed her.

Elena spotted Lexi immediately. "Oh goodness, you must be Natala's sister. You look just like her!" She exclaimed as she bent down to give Lexi a hug. "It's so nice to meet you. And who is this adorable bundle of fur?"

"That's Daisy," Drew supplied as he watched Elena coo over the golden retriever. "She's Lexi's partner in crime."

"She looks like the most adorable partner to have." Elena smiled at Lexi.

"Did you start the party already?" Natala asked as she stepped out onto the deck, followed closely by Tony. Elena immediately ran over to give her a hug.

"How could we start without you?" Drew asked his sister. "It's your brunch thing."

"You couldn't," Natala replied sweetly. "You both met Elena? She just moved back to the States last month."

Drew gave her a curious look. "Where were you living before that?" He asked her.

Elena laughed and gathered her hair into a ponytail, something Drew watched with interest. "Rome," she replied. "I was nannying a family there, but now their children are all in school and they've decided to just find a housekeeper instead." She wrinkled her nose. "I love children and nannying. I will happily clean up after the children, but I'm not the housekeeper type. So, I moved back here because Tony seems to have settled. I'll be looking for a new family to nanny." She smiled; her hair now neatly pulled back. "Have you ever been to Italy?"

"I haven't," Drew replied, sitting down in one of the chairs as he spoke.

"You should visit sometime; it is such a beautiful country," Elena told him as she selected the chair beside his and sat down.

"That's for sure. I can't wait to go back," Natala said, watching the pair carefully. Drew wondered what she was seeing.

"When are you leaving?" Lexi asked. She backed up in her wheelchair as Connie ran past her back into the house.

"Tonight. That way we can sleep on the plane and enjoy all the sights when we get there," Natala answered, meeting Tony's eyes.

"It's so adorable you two are going back to Italy for your honeymoon. It's such a full circle moment! You met there and fell in love there, now you are going back together to celebrate your marriage," Elena gushed.

"Food is ready!" Connie called as she came back outside, setting a plate of bacon down on the table.

"That bacon is for me. I'm not sure what you are going to eat," Lexi told Drew as she reached for the bacon.

"Alexica," Connie warned.

Lexi looked at Drew and raised her eyebrows.

Drew shrugged, glancing at Connie before looking back at Lexi. "Nerves," he whispered to his twin by way of explanation. "She doesn't know what to do now that her oldest daughter is married."

"And she's worried about the flight, and Natala being in Italy. It's a good thing she didn't know the first time." Lexi replied, taking two pieces of bacon before passing the plate to Drew.

Drew took a single strip of bacon as he glanced at the muffins. "What can I have Mom?" He asked Connie.

Connie smiled. "Everything on the table is gluten-free, have whatever you want. The Kringle I got to have after Natala and Tony open gifts is not gluten-free though."

Drew noddled, then took a chocolate muffin from one of the baskets and used a knife to cut it open.

"Are you allergic to gluten?" Elena asked as she also took a chocolate muffin.

"Yep," Drew replied as he buttered his muffin. "Have been for years. I'm used to it now."

"There are so many things made gluten-free nowadays I wouldn't think it is that difficult." Elena paused. "Expensive, yes, but not hard. In Italy, most of the restaurants have at least one gluten-free option."

"Interesting." Drew filed that piece of information away, just in case. He didn't really intend to travel anytime soon, but it would be great to go somewhere he'd have many food options.

He watched as Elena buttered her muffin, then took a small bite. She closed her eyes and smiled, a simple thing, yet at this moment it seemed seductive.

Her eyes popped open, and she looked at Connie. "Thank you for making brunch, Mrs. Luna. These muffins are delicious. The chocolate flavor is so strong."

Connie beamed. "Thank you, Elena. Chocolate is one of Natala's favorite things, so I've had plenty of practice."

"Coffee," Natala whispered to Elena from across the table. "The secret is that she adds a little bit of coffee to the batter. It brings out all the chocolate flavor."

"Coffee!" Connie exclaimed. "I forgot about that; I have coffee ready if anyone would like any. And there is orange juice. I should bring that out too." She jumped out of her chair and disappeared into the house.

Drew looked at Lexi and they both laughed. "Nerves," Lexi agreed. "She always gets forgetful when she's nervous."

After brunch had been eaten, the leftovers packed up, and the dishes washed; it was finally time for presents to be opened. Drew was surprised to see there was a large stack of them in the living room. He had opted for the gift card route. It seemed like a much easier wedding gift. And, it was a lot more portable than these other things.

"What could that be? It's heavy." Drew asked no one in particular, pointing to the tall and skinny box that was leaning against the wall.

"Furniture is my guess," Elena replied, looking at the box carefully. "Especially if it is heavy. I think it is a table or shelf or something. It's not prebuilt, so it will be a test to see if Natala and Tony can build furniture together." She sat down on the floor beside Daisy.

"Furniture would make sense," Drew agreed as he claimed a spot on the couch.

"Okay, Natala and Tony, make sure to read who the gift is from before you open it." Connie instructed, sitting down beside the couple and their gifts. "I'll write that down along with what it is, so the thank you notes can be written."

Natala smiled, her eyes sparkling as she looked over at her siblings. "Anyone else getting flashbacks to birthday parties?" She asked with a laugh.

"Definitely," Lexi replied, watching her mother balance the notebook on her knee. "Except this is a lot quieter than those birthday parties ever were."

"True," Natala agreed, picking up a small box. "Okay Mom, this one is from Auntie Ruth..."

Drew tried to pay attention to the gifts that were being opened, but he found himself distracted by Elena. That distraction doubled when she sat down next to him after the first few gifts had been opened.

"That's going to be a machine of some sort," Elena whispered as Tony struggled to pick up a box. "It's heavy and not small, I'm guessing a coffee machine."

"A microwave?" Drew offered, noticing that Elena smelled like raspberries.

"Too heavy. Besides, microwaves come with apartments. They wouldn't need one of those," Elena replied as they both watched Natala carefully open the gift. Drew had to say Natala was one of the slowest gift openers he had ever met. Right now, it was very annoying.

"A toaster oven!" Natala exclaimed after she pulled away the last of the wrapping paper. "It's so cute, that will be so handy." She handed the box to Tony.

"One of the guys I met last year on my cross-country photo trip had one of these in his van," Tony explained. "Told me it's basically a mini-oven; you can use it for all the same things. It will be a great kitchen tool to have. I can't wait to use it."

"I was closer," Drew whispered to Elena. "It heats things up just like a microwave does."

"You were closer. I want to point out that it would work to make coffee too, but I don't really know how it could." Elena replied softly as they watched Natala pick up the next box.

"She's lifting it like there is nothing inside. I'm guessing pillows," Drew said, watching as Natala read the tag to their mother.

"Too small for pillows," Elena argued, her hair brushing against Drew's cheek as she tried to get a closer look. "Technically, it could be small pillows, but I don't think they had any of those on their registry. I'm guessing it's towels."

"Towels are heavier than pillows," Drew pointed out, trying to ignore the silky hair. He watched as Natala began to take the paper off the box.

They watched as Natala opened the box and smiled. "That's so cute!" She exclaimed as she pulled out a small pillow. The front was embroidered to say "Antonio and Natala Calo" along with their wedding date.

"That's a keepsake for sure!" Connie exclaimed as she scribbled something down in her notebook.

"I'll get the next one," Elena said, leaning forward to watch as Tony selected another box.

Drew and Elena guessed gifts throughout the rest of the gift opening, sometimes getting them right and sometimes being very wrong. Drew missed the suspicious glances Lexi kept sending his way.

"Thank you everyone, for coming to brunch. And for all you did for the wedding," Natala said as she hung on to her husband's arm. "And thanks Dad, for agreeing to move all of this stuff to our apartment while we are gone."

David gave his oldest daughter a hug. "That's what dads are for. Have fun in Italy."

"Drew." Lexi put her hand on his arm, carefully pulling him away from Elena.

Drew followed her outside, where she raised her eyebrows at him. "Why her? You've gone through so many girlfriends I can't even keep track. She can't be your next. She's Tony's only family, from what I know. She will probably be around on holidays and such. Please don't make anything weird. We just got Natala back, I don't want to lose her."

"Lexi, we are all adults here. Let it be. It's some harmless flirting. I'm not going to ask for her number. The only way I'll see her again is during those holidays you're worried about." Drew folded his arms across his chest.

Lexi's hands hovered over the wheels of her chair. "Just be careful," she said with a sigh, beginning to wheel away. "That's all I'm saying."

"Noted," Drew replied as he followed her back into the house. "I'm heading home Mom. I'll see you before too long."

"Drive safely," Connie replied absentmindedly as she studied the notebook on her lap. "I wonder if I should start writing these out for Natala. That would..."

Drew hightailed it out of the house before his mom could ask for help with the thank-you notes. He'd had enough of the wedding stuff. As he began walking back to his house, his phone buzzed in his pocket.

He fished it out, noting the animal shelter was calling. They probably had a new dog that needed a foster home.

"Hello?" He answered, looking both ways before crossing the street.

"Drew, I wouldn't be calling if I had any other choice." Gabi – the shelter's foster coordinator – was speaking a lot faster than she normally did. "All our normal fosters are full, and this sweet girl was just found. She's very shy and skittish, so she really needs to be in a home with no other animals."

"I have to do a quick clean of my house. I definitely left some of my papers out in the living room. But I can help out. Do you want to bring her or should I pick her up?" Drew frowned. "What breed is she, big or small dog?"

Gabi paused. "That's the thing." She said finally, as Drew balanced his phone on his shoulder to unlock his front door. "It's not a dog, it's a cat."

Drew's phone clattered to the ground and his front door swung open. He grabbed the phone and gave it a quick glance to make sure nothing had cracked. "I'm sorry Gabi. I could swear I heard you say it was a cat."

"That's because I did," Gabi replied slowly. "Like I said earlier, I wouldn't be asking if I didn't have to. She needs a place for a little while, so she can get a little more comfortable with people. She was surrendered by an elderly lady who couldn't take care of her any longer, and she's pretty skinny."

"I don't know anything about cats," Drew said, dropping his keys on the countertop, then taking off his shoes. "I've only ever fostered dogs."

Gabi sighed. "There's a family that could probably take her when they get back from vacation, but that's a week away. Can you at least take her for a week? I'll grab the books we have on cats; you can read all you need to know."

Silently, Drew shook his head. None of the manuals he'd gotten on fostering dogs had prepared him, so he doubted the cat books would be any better. "How long until you are bringing her over?" He asked with a sigh of his own.

"Thank you." He could hear the relief in Gabi's voice. "I'll bring her over in an hour. I have a crate for her, so you won't need that. And I'll bring enough food for a couple of days."

"See you in an hour," Drew replied, then hung up the phone. He sighed again as he sat it down beside his keys. What did he know about cats? Especially a nervous cat. How could he be any help in this situation?

After doing a quick clean of the living room and kitchen, Drew sat down on the couch and grabbed his laptop. He typed "fostering cats, what I need to know, " into the search engine and began to read.

Chapter 3

Drew quickly learned that when Gabi had said she had the cat wasn't sociable or friendly; she wasn't kidding. The only glimpse he'd had of the calico cat was when Gabi had opened the cat carrier and let her out. Pebbles – which Drew thought was a very odd name for a cat – had quickly claimed a spot under his couch and did not want to come out.

"I have food for you." Drew offered, setting the bowl in front of the couch. He backed away as quietly as he could, trying to hear if the cat moved at all.

With a sigh, he walked back to the kitchen and began to make his own dinner. Make was a generous term, really it was reheating. His mom made sure he was always well stocked on meals, so all he had to do was microwave.

Drew checked his email as he ate some lasagna, quickly deleting all the spam emails. For whatever reason, he seemed to have plenty of those, even through the school email. Nothing he actually needed, so he could put his phone down for the rest of the night.

He took another bite of lasagna, then froze with the dish still on his fork. *There was a noise, was that the cat bowl moving?* Drew moved as slowly as possible to look into the living room. He didn't want to scare the poor cat, but he wanted to make sure she was okay.

Sure enough, now that he'd distanced himself, Pebbles had come out of the couch a bit and was eating her dinner. *At least she's eating,* Drew thought. *I may have to move the litter box a little closer to the couch.*

He'd set it up in the bathroom, something the internet had recommended. The internet had also recommended that he show the cat the litter box, something he hadn't been able to do. Drew did not want to clean under the couch if the cat decided that was her bathroom.

After he finished his dinner and washed the dishes, Drew peeked into the living room. Pebbles had once again disappeared under the couch, as Drew had expected. He moved the litter box from the bathroom to the living room where the cat could see it, talking to her the entire time. Maybe she'd be more comfortable if she got used to his voice.

"Do you like television?" Drew asked the cat as he sat down on the couch. "I'm going to turn it on. It's going to make noise." He frowned, remembering that Gabi had said Pebbles used to live with an old lady. *Old ladies watched a lot of tv, didn't they? Maybe television would be familiar to the cat.*

Drew turned on the screen and flipped channels until he found a game show to watch, then sat back. He heard a car door slam. A quick glance next door revealed that Cameron had gotten home. From the looks of it, he wasn't in the best of spirits. *Working a twelve-hour shift would do that to you,* Drew reasoned. His long days during parent-teacher conferences were never great. At least he got to sit down. Nursing seemed like a lot of being on your feet.

"Tomato." Drew told the television when it asked for food people didn't realize was a fruit. "Peppers."

***

Thankfully, the next day was a Sunday, so Drew could sleep in a little bit. Unfortunately, that meant Gabi wasn't working at the shelter today. Drew had driven out there hoping that someone would have advice for him. Pebbles still refused to come out from under the couch.

"She's eating, but the bowl is right beside the couch. And she won't come out to eat unless I'm out of sight," Drew explained to Esther, the receptionist. Usually when he saw Esther, it was to drop off a dog he'd been fostering that had a new home awaiting him or her.

"I'm glad she's eating, that's huge," Esther said as she pulled open one of the drawers on her filing cabinet. "She looked very skinny yesterday, so really I don't know how much eating she had been able to do in the past," she trailed off and shrugged as she looked through the files, then pulled one out.

"Here is her file. Let's see if there is anything else that could make her more comfortable." As Drew leaned against the countertop behind the desk, Esther sat back down and set the file down.

"Older lady, like you remembered." A sad look came over Esther's face as she read. "The daughter brought Pebbles in. It seems she's taking her mom to live with her and is allergic to cats. That's too bad for both Pebbles and her owner."

Drew crossed his arms over his chest, unsure what to say or how that would help him.

"Be patient with the little kitty," Esther advised, still looking at the file. "There's nothing else here that could be helpful." She closed the file and turned her chair, so she was facing Drew. "I'd suggest trying to move her food a little further from the couch every time you feed her. Gradually get her out a tiny bit more."

"That's simple enough," Drew replied. "I've been talking to her a lot. Seems weird to do when I can't see her."

Esther's face brightened. "That's a great idea," she said with a smile. "You could also get a sweatshirt or something that you've worn for a couple hours – something that smells like you. If you put that near the couch, it may help her get used to your smell. Especially when you are at school this week. But I'd caution you against actually putting it under the couch. She seems to have claimed that as her safe space so you want to keep it that way."

"That makes sense. So, food further and further," Drew pulled out his phone and opened the notes app, starting to type as he spoke. "Keep talking to her, and a sweatshirt that smells like me." He paused, then added let the couch be her safe space to the list. "Thank you, Esther. Cats really aren't my wheelhouse. Are you sure you don't want to foster her?"

Esther smiled at him. "You never know what animal is going to steal your heart," She replied knowingly, a sparkle in her eye. "And try not to think of Pebbles as just a cat, she's unique and special just like any of the dogs you've fostered."

Drew put his phone back in his pocket. "Noted." He grinned. "I'll try it all out, and if I have any luck, I won't be back until that family finishes their vacation."

Esther shrugged, a smile still on her face as the phone rang. "Happy Tails and Scales Rescue, how can I help you?" She answered.

Drew glanced at the puppies in a kennel near the door. "You are all so cute. I should tell Cameron about you. He and Lexi are talking about getting another dog," he told them as he gave some pets through the kennel walls.

Drew walked over to the door, but before he could open it, a woman came running into him. "Woah." He said, steadying her.

"I'm sorry." The woman squeaked, glancing out the door.

Drew let go of her and backed up, then frowned as he noticed the long, black hair. "Elena?" He asked.

She whirled around, her eyes wide. They relaxed a bit when she realized who he was. "Andrew."

Drew looked at her with a frown, noting her face was flushed as if she'd been running and she had a nervous expression. "What's going on?"

Elena smiled and glanced out the door again. "Nothing," she replied, then looked around the building. Her eyes lit up as she spotted the puppies. "Oh, my goodness, you are all absolutely adorable." She cooed as she walked over to the kennel and petted them.

Drew blinked, glancing out the door himself in case that could answer any questions. *Why was Elena here, at an animal shelter? Why did it seem like she had been running?*

"Hello! I'm Esther, and these are some of our newest guests. Half German Shepherd and half husky. They are definitely going to be some big dogs when they are all grown up." Ester walked over to Elena and opened one of the kennel doors.

Drew looked at them for a moment, then remembered the conversation he and Lexi had had yesterday. Or more accurately, the lecture Lexi had given him. He opened the door and walked outside, glancing around the parking lot but seeing nothing out of the ordinary.

He unlocked his car and slid into the driver's seat, chalking it all up to a weird coincidence. Or fever dream, but he was pretty sure he wasn't dreaming. The notes app on his phone still held all the advice he'd gotten from Esther.

Oh well, not my problem. Drew thought as he backed out of the parking spot. Elena wasn't related to him. She wasn't dating him, wasn't his responsibility. If she had some kind of trouble, surely her brother would be aware and help her.

Besides, he only had a little bit of his weekend left, then it would be back to school. Drew was looking forward to taking a jog around the neighborhood before his afternoon nap.

***

The jog went just as Drew had planned, but his nap was interrupted by a visitor. "Lexi," Drew greeted as he opened the door for his sister and Daisy. "I have a foster right now. Keep Daisy close to you please."

Lexi smiled. "You do? What breed this time, a lab maybe? It's been a while since you've fostered a lab. Or a golden. Something close to Daisy's size."

Drew groaned, knowing Lexi was going to remember this forever. He closed the door behind her and Daisy. He didn't want Pebbles to get out. Not that she'd choose to leave the couch, but he wasn't taking any chances.

"Not exactly," he replied, walking over to the kitchen and opening the fridge. He pulled out two bottles of water and set them on the counter. As Lexi settled herself and Daisy in the living room, he opened one of them and chugged it.

He handed one to Lexi, then sat down on the couch.

"So where is the dog?" Lexi asked, looking around. Drew could see the moment she noticed the litter box, because her eyebrows moved together in a frown. "Dogs don't normally use litter boxes," she said, staring at her brother.

Drew took the last sip of water from his bottle, relishing the coolness as it went down his throat. "That might be because my new foster isn't a dog."

Lexi's eyebrows rose as she watched Drew to see if he was serious. After a moment she began to giggle. "Really Drew?" She asked between giggles. "A cat? You claimed that you'd never ever let a cat enter this house."

"Yeah, yeah, yeah, laugh all you want. She needed a place to stay, I have a house."

"Oh, poor Drew, you didn't know how to say no." Lexi put her hand on her heart as she tried to stop laughing, something that seemed to be very difficult for her. Finally, she took a sip of her water. "Gabi always knew how to get to you."

Drew shook his head. "She had nothing to do with it," he argued. He and Gabi had dated for a couple months. It had been fun, but then Gabi had found someone else and that was it.

She'd gotten him to foster a dog, claiming it would just be once. Now he was in his third year of fostering.

"So, where is the cat?" Lexi asked, sitting back in her wheelchair. "You already have it? Or has it not arrived yet?"

"She is under the couch," Drew explained, shaking his head. "Pebbles, that's her name. She ran under the couch as soon as she got here and hasn't really come out."

"Oh, poor kitty," Lexi cooed, setting her bottle on an end table. She slid off her wheelchair to the floor, peeking her head under the couch. "There's a blob under here, is that you Pebbles?" She asked.

Drew raised his eyebrows. He should have guessed Lexi wouldn't mind the cat; she loved animals, always had. But maybe that was because she had more patience than anyone else he knew.

"She's big," Lexi said as she sat up on the floor. "And not moving."

"I thought you weren't supposed to comment on a woman's size."

"Andrew." Lexi shot daggers at him with her eyes. "You knew what I meant."

Drew shrugged, leaning back in his chair. He should have just ignored the door. "Why are you here instead of working or something at home?" He changed the subject.

Lexi bit her lip, a habit his sisters shared. "Mom was having a very loud conversation with a client. Maybe it was an argument. Either way, I really couldn't concentrate. I don't have that much work to do right now anyway."

"It's Sunday, I thought Mom didn't work on Sundays." Drew commented, glancing at the calendar to make sure there wasn't anything written.

"I don't know. It's someone important or something, I'm not sure exactly. Don't really want to know. Dad is at the shop for a couple more hours, so I figured I'd come over here." She glanced at the house next door, likely giving away more than she intended to.

"Cameron's working a twelve again?" Drew asked, not really needing confirmation.

"Yeah." Lexi sighed. "He's been moved to the ER. It's not an easy place to work."

That explained the slamming of the car door last night. "Is that a temporary move? Or will he stay for a while?"

"Temporary. Two weeks, eleven shifts. All twelves." Lexi answered. She lay down on the floor and peeked under the couch again. "Pebbles, why don't you come out from under the couch?" She asked the cat. "I'll pet you."

"Daisy, she's betraying you," Drew told the dog dryly.

Daisy's tail wagged as she lay down beside Lexi's empty wheelchair.

"She doesn't care," Lexi replied. "She knows I love her. That's not betrayal."

Drew shook his head and stood up. "I need a shower. Good luck with the cat." He dropped the empty water bottle in the recycling, then walked down the hall to his room.

He grabbed some clothes that weren't covered in sweat, then walked into the bathroom. After he took a quick shower and got dressed, he glanced around his bedroom, unsure where his phone ended up. He checked the pocket of the sweatshirt he'd been wearing, noting it was empty.

"Lexi, can you call my phone?" Drew called as he walked down the hall. "I can't find it."

"Shush!" Lexi squealed, and Drew watched a bolt of fur dash back under the couch as he entered the living room. "Drew, she was on my lap."

"Really?" Drew asked, wondering how Lexi had managed that. He walked into the kitchen and checked the countertops, not seeing his phone anywhere.

"Yes. You scared her off, probably by talking too loudly." Lexi's eyes narrowed as she watched Drew search the living room. "Have you tried being quieter? Maybe that's why Pebbles is scared, you are too loud."

Drew paused his search for a moment. "Maybe," he agreed, deciding to just accept Lexi's rude comment about his noise levels. "I guess the older lady she lived with probably wasn't a loud person."

"She also moved a lot slower; I'd guess." Lexi noted as Drew pulled up one of the couch cushions. "What are you looking for?"

"My phone, I said that before." Drew gave her a pointed look. "The search would likely go faster if you could call it."

Lexi rolled her eyes, but pulled out her phone and dialed Drew's number. When they heard the buzzing, Drew walked to the door and picked it up off the floor. "How did it get there?" He asked.

Lexi hung up the call. "I don't know," she replied.

"You think this is funny," Drew accused, watching the smile on her face.

Lexi laughed. "Kind of, yeah. All of it, your phone on the floor and the cat. I thought you hated cats."

"I just am not a fan," Drew corrected. "And it's only for a week, then there will be a new place for her to go."

Lexi glanced at the couch. "Poor girl," she murmured. "She's going to have so much change."

Drew slipped his phone into his pocket. "Your boyfriend is home."

Lexi looked out the window, her eyes brightening. "He is," she replied, picking up Daisy's leash. "Come on Daisy, let's go over there. Good luck with the cat Drew."

"Sure." Drew replied as the front door closed behind Lexi. "I could use a whole lot of that."

He looked at the couch, remembering Esther's advice. He walked down the hall to his room and picked up the sweatshirt, then brought it back to the living room and set it down beside the couch.

"There Pebbles. That's what I smell like. Does it help to know that? I'll be gone all day tomorrow, maybe you'll explore the house some more then." *I'll have to make sure some doors are closed so she can't get into any trouble.*

Chapter 4

"So, now that everyone has learned what a circle graph is," Drew walked in front of his sixth-grade class, eyeing each of them.

They had the Monday afternoon blues, that was for sure. Not that he was a huge fan of Mondays either, and he did have to admit this last period seemed like it was going on forever.

"I have a homework assignment for you," he continued.

As the children groaned, he felt himself smile. "Come on guys, this one is going to be fun."

"Mr. Luna, homework is never fun."

Drew chuckled as he leaned against his desk. "Francis, maybe this will be the first homework assignment you find fun." He shrugged. "I'm asking for each of you to come up with a question, and four possible answers." He walked over to the whiteboards and uncapped a marker.

As he wrote on the board, he spoke. "For instance, let's say I asked the question, 'What is the best ice cream flavor?'" Drew added the numbers one through four underneath that question. "I'm going to pick four possible answers, so let's say chocolate, vanilla, mint, and strawberry." He capped the marker again and set it down.

"You can come up with your own question, food related or not." Drew grinned at his class. "And this is the fun part. I want you to take this question to at least twenty unique people. Teachers, classmates, family, the clerk at the grocery store. I don't care who you ask. Once you have asked twenty – or more – people, I want you to make a circle graph of your results." Drew grabbed a new marker and drew a circle on the board beside his question.

"You all have a week for this assignment, and I urge you to ask as many people as you can – gather as much data as you can. Have fun with it!" Drew's last word was drowned out as the bell rang and his students gathered their things.

Francis was one of the last to leave and made her way to Drew's desk. "Can I make my graph about video games?" She asked him eagerly.

Drew laughed and shrugged. "Sure, go ahead. But keep in mind you need to ask twenty people, so you need to have twenty people with an opinion on that topic."

Francis frowned for a moment, then smiled. "Okay," she replied, then ran out of the classroom to catch up with her friends.

Drew packed up his things, wondering what sort of question Francis was going to be asking people. This was one of his favorite assignments to give each year, because the kids got some freedom with it. It was always fun to see what questions the kids came up with.

"Are you going to be seeing Lexi?"

Drew looked up, still trying to stuff his laptop into its bag. Birdie was standing in his classroom doorway, holding a manila envelope. "I don't have any specific plans but I'm sure I will. You have something for her?"

"Receipts." Birdie set the envelope on his desk with a sheepish smile. "They are backdated a couple months; I haven't exactly been great at getting them to her on time."

Drew smiled and added that envelope to his bag. "You are having me take them to her, because she won't get mad at me?"

"Exactly." Birdie confirmed with a smile. "Thanks Drew, you're the best!" She called as she walked out of the room.

Drew shook his head and zipped up his bag, then slung it over his shoulder. He grabbed his keys and coffee cup, then turned off the classroom lights. As he walked through the halls, there were still some kids around, but most of them had already caught the bus and left.

He made it to his car without interacting with anyone, something that seemed very appropriate for a Monday. Drew set his bag in the passenger seat, coffee cup in the cup holder, then put his keys in the ignition.

After starting the car, he pulled his phone out of his pocket and opened up the nanny cam app he'd installed. It was a great way to keep track of his fosters when he was at work. This time, however, it wasn't the most helpful. Pebbles seemed to be staying under the couch.

Drew sighed and put the phone in his second cup holder and began driving. *I'll stop at the pet store,* he decided. *All the toys and treats I have are for dogs. Maybe if I got some for cats, Pebbles would be more interested.*

Drew was no stranger to the local pet store. He often went after getting a new foster, usually taking the dog along to pick out a toy of their own. *Do people take cats to pet stores?* He wondered as he pulled into the parking lot. He'd never seen a cat walking around the store with their owner. Pebbles wouldn't have come with him anyway.

He locked his car and walked into the store, bypassing his usual aisles of dog toys.

"Drew?"

"Hey Kenzie," he greeted the store employee. This pet store wasn't a chain, it was a small local store that Kenzie and her mom owned. One of the reasons it was Drew's favorite place for anything dog related. Or in this case, cat related. "Do you know anything about cats?"

Kenzie grinned. "Of course. Are you fostering a cat?" She asked, leading him to the cat aisle.

"For a week, I guess. I don't know much about cats and I have no toys or treats," he told her, looking at the cat toys. They all seemed so tiny.

"This one is a great choice if you are looking for entertainment you don't have to be a part of." Kenzie picked up what looked like a large plastic circle. Upon further inspection, Drew saw there was a ball inside the tube.

"The cat can get their paw in that slot and push the ball around." Kenzie shrugged. "I don't know why it entertains them, but it does." She pulled another toy off a shelf and handed it to Drew. "This is more for you to play with the cat, a mouse attached to a wand. It also comes with an extra mouse; the cat can play with that one on their own."

She turned to the other side of the aisle. "As for treats, I'd recommend these." Kenzie added a small plastic jar to Drew's arms. "They are most popular with the cat owners that come here, and they are pretty small."

Drew looked at his arms. He hadn't thought it would be this easy, or quick. Maybe he should try asking for help more often. "Great, I'll just get all of this then."

As he walked to the checkout counter, he noticed a cat bed. He grabbed that as well; it was small enough to fit under the couch if that was where Pebbles wanted it.

Drew paid for his purchases and thanked Kenzie.

Kenzie smiled as she handed him the paper bag. "Thank you for shopping! We will see you next time."

Drew hoped next time he'd be coming back for dog supplies, but he didn't voice that thought. He opened the door and began making his way to his car when someone ran into him, almost knocking him backwards.

"Careful," Drew said, trying to steady himself. He frowned at the familiar raspberry smell. "Elena?" He asked. Was it really her, or was this déjà vu? The same thing had happened yesterday.

Elena backed away; her eyes wide. "Drew," she gasped out.

Drew looked at her, concerned. "Where are you going?" He asked, looking around the parking lot.

Elena glanced behind her, then shook her head. "Anywhere, I need to..." She trailed off. "Just not be here."

"I'm going back to my house, if you want to come with me." Drew offered. He wasn't sure what else to do. He couldn't call Tony. Besides the fact that he didn't have the man's number, he and Natala were still on their honeymoon.

"Yes, please." Elena looked relieved as she followed Drew to his car.

Drew grabbed his bag and moved it to the back of the car so Elena could have the passenger seat. *Was this a crazy coincidence? She'd run into him – literally – twice now. What were the odds of that?*

Elena got into the car quickly and buckled her seatbelt, then ducked down in the seat so no one could see her if they walked by.

Drew got into his own seat, silently wondering what the girl was hiding from. She had to be hiding from something. No sane person acted like this unless something was seriously wrong. Her face was red and her eyes were wide with fear.

Neither Drew nor Elena said anything as Drew drove. Elena didn't even look up from her lap until Drew's garage door closed behind the car. He got out of the car and opened the back door, gathering his bags. "Come inside. I promise I won't bite."

Elena carefully unbuckled her seatbelt and got out of the car, taking a deep breath.

Drew was relieved to see some of the fear leave her face. He unlocked the door, turning on the lights in the house. "Welcome to my house. It's not much," he said as Elena followed him inside.

Drew set his bag onto one of the barstools, then took the paper bag over to the living room. "I'm fostering a cat right now, and she seems to have claimed the underside of the couch as her home," he explained.

Elena sat down on a chair, looking at the couch curiously. Drew pulled the bed out of the bag, wondering how Elena could be this quiet. The first two times he'd met her, she seemed so bubbly and energetic.

"Pebbles, I got you a bed," he informed the cat, carefully setting it beside the couch.

He also pulled out the ring toy, and set that on the floor in case the cat wanted to come out and explore.

"There's really a cat under there?" Elena asked with a frown. "Are you sure it isn't just your imagination?"

"Look for yourself," Drew invited, laying down on the floor so he could see under the couch. The ball of fur was still there.

Elena lay down on her stomach beside him and peered under the couch. "There is a cat," she stated with surprise in her voice. "Here kitty-kitty," she cooed.

To Drew's surprise, Pebbles glanced over at Elena with interest. He frowned. "That's strange," he said slowly. "She came out of the couch yesterday, when Lexi was here."

"Maybe she does better with females," Elena offered, slowly sticking her hand closer to the cat.

Drew watched as Pebbles didn't back away further, then slowly stood up. "Maybe. Let's try that theory out," he replied, walking over to the kitchen where Pebbles couldn't see him. He sat down on the barstool and unpacked his bag from work, trying not to pay attention to Elena.

He pulled out his phone and sent a quick text to Lexi, letting her know he had receipts for her. As he set his phone down, he glanced over at Elena. Somehow, Pebbles had her little head peeking out from under the couch. She was sniffing Elena's hand, then letting Elena pet her.

Drew frowned, wondering if the cat had ever had a male in her life. *How old was the cat anyway?* He hadn't bothered to ask Gabi. If she was a young cat, maybe the elderly lady was all she'd known.

"She's sweet," Elena commented as Pebbles climbed into her lap. "And beautiful, I love calico cats. Did you know almost all calico cats are female? It's a really, really low percentage of them that are male."

"I think I've heard that before," Drew replied, watching Elena pet the cat. "Cats aren't something I know much about; I've always fostered dogs."

"You're missing out." Elena smiled at the cat. "Dogs are quick to please; cats are different. You have to earn their respect. I like that about them."

Drew stood up, watching to see if Pebbles would bolt. She turned to watch him, but she didn't move from Elena's lap. "Keep talking. I'm going to try to very slowly get closer to you," he told Elena.

"That's a good idea. Pebbles, how did you get that name? Is it from the cereal? Or the television show?" Elena continued to pet the cat as Drew took tiny steps towards the pair. "I had a calico cat that looked like you when I was little, her name was Barbie."

"Barbie?" Drew asked, raising his eyebrow.

Elena looked up from the cat and laughed. "Yes, Barbie. I was five when we got her. I loved my barbies."

"Have you had a cat, or any pet, since?" Drew asked. He was about a yard away from Pebbles and Elena, and Pebbles started to look nervous. He sat down on the floor, trying not to move too fast and startle the cat.

"No, I haven't. I didn't really have the time for a pet, nannying took most of my time. I had a guesthouse on the property, but I wasn't there for much other than sleep. It would have been unfair to them." Elena explained, looking down and smiling at Pebbles.

"This is the second time you've run into me, literally," Drew frowned. "In two days."

Elena blushed, not meeting Drew's gaze. "I'm sorry about that," she replied, picking up the toy Drew had set on the floor earlier and showing it to Pebbles.

"What are you running from Elena?" Drew asked, watching her carefully. She still wouldn't look at him, she was definitely hiding something.

"It's nothing. I've got it handled." Elena looked unsure of herself, contrary to her words. "It's just a man."

A boyfriend? Drew wondered. "A man?"

Elena took a deep breath, shaking the toy for pebbles. It sounded like there was a bell inside the toy somewhere. "Since I was like sixteen, there has been a man following me."

Drew raised his eyebrows, unsure how he was supposed to respond to that. "Since you were sixteen? How long is that?" He asked her. The use of the word "like" also made him curious, but he didn't want to ask too many questions.

Elena laughed. "I'm almost twenty-four," she replied, "So around eight years?" She grimaced. "Off and on though. I moved to Italy when I turned eighteen and he didn't follow me there. Well, at least not much."

"Not much? Not much is from different than not at all. Do you know who the man is, or why he is following you?" Drew frowned, trying to piece together this puzzle in his head.

"When Natala was there – in Italy – I thought I saw him. I'm not sure if it was the same man or not. He had a beard then, and he never has in America. I guess that could have been my imagination. But now, since I got back from Italy, it's definitely the same man that followed me when I was younger. It's like I go into a place, and when I leave, he is there watching me." Elena reached for her hair and wound it into a bun, carefully grabbing a ponytail holder from her wrist to secure it.

"I don't have a clue who he is or what he wants. I'd never seen him before. Then, in high school, I realized he always seemed to be there at the end of the day. He followed me home one day, and the day after that, until I started riding the bus. Even then, he'd be watching me get onto the bus."

"Did you tell anyone? Your parents? Your brother?" Drew stood up, startling Pebbles. She ran back under the couch as he walked over to the fridge.

"My mom wasn't really around; she'd gotten married again by that time and was always out with her new husband. I've never known him well enough to tell him anything." Elena sighed. "My dad died a bit before it started, so I couldn't tell him. And Tony knows, he helped me get a job in Italy and move there to get away from him." She glanced under the couch for Pebbles.

Drew pulled two bottles of sparkling cranberry juice from the fridge. "Juice?" He asked Elena.

She smiled. "Sure."

He opened both bottles before walking over to the living room. He handed Elena one of them, then sat down on the ouch. "Have you ever gone to the police about it?"

"Yes." Elena replied, slowly getting up from the floor, then sitting beside Drew on the couch. "They told me I was imagining things. Recommended that I speak with my doctor, because it could be anxiety."

"That's crazy, they should have at least investigated. Followed you for a day to see if the man was there or something. Maybe things are changed, you should try reporting it now." Elena was sitting close enough to him Drew could smell the raspberry scent she seemed to have. He took a sip of juice, trying to distract himself.

Elena shrugged, her shoulder brushing his. "I'll think about it," she replied, looking at the bottle of juice in her hand. "Sparkling cranberry juice?"

"It has always been my mom's favorite drink. She says she doesn't drink wine, but she drinks plenty of sparkling cranberry juice I guess it's a habit now for my sisters and I to drink it," Drew explained.

Elena tried a sip, then smiled. "I've had cranberry juice before, but never sparkling. I don't know why I've never tried it before, it's really good. You have good taste."

"Lots of people would disagree with you there. I eat gluten-free and I actually enjoy it." Drew leaned back, watching Elena. She was looking right back at him, her hazel eyes seeming to see into his soul.

Drew suddenly felt like he was getting in too deep. There was something about Elena that was intoxicating, he couldn't stay away from her.

"You really need to go to Italy. There are plenty of options there and very good ones as well. I've tried some of them, there's a little hole in the wall that serves a gluten-free margarita pizza and it is absolutely to die for." Elena's hands moved as she talked, something Drew found fascinating.

Although he seemed to find everything Elena did fascinating. Why was that? Normally he was the one the girls chased, not the other way around.

He tried to distract himself. "We have margarita pizza in the States. I just got a gluten-free one from the grocery store last week, it's made with a cauliflower crust."

Elena looked absolutely horrified. "Cauliflower crust?" She asked slowly.

"Don't hate it until you've tried it. It gets too much hate." Drew glanced at the clock, realizing it was getting close to dinner time. The sandwich he'd eaten during the lunch period seemed so long ago.

"What are your plans for the rest of the day? Do you want to stick around and try the pizza?"

"I don't really have anything planned." Elena looked out the window. Looking for the man stalking her, Drew suspected.

"Sure, I'll stay. But I make no promise that my opinion of the pizza will change after trying it. Pizza crust is special, it shouldn't be messed with."

Drew chuckled and got up from the couch. "Just wait till you try it," he said. "And hey, maybe Pebbles will come back out while I'm in the kitchen."

Elena's eyes brightened as if she'd forgotten about Pebbles for a moment. "You have a cat and you're cooking for me. I may never leave," she blurted out, then blushed. "I mean..." she trailed off and gave a nervous giggle.

Drew met her eyes, feeling as if there was electricity between them. "Start the pizza," he said aloud, trying to remind himself what he was doing.

"You start the pizza, and I'll try to make friends with Pebbles," Elena replied, sliding to the floor so she could peer under the couch.

Chapter 5

It was dark outside when Drew heard a knock on the door. "I can get it." Elena gave him a smile, hopping up from the barstool. "Since you're the one doing all the work here – cooking, cleaning."

"Thanks," Drew replied as he grabbed the washcloth and wiped the plate, making sure to get all the pizza sauce off it. Elena hadn't admitted that she liked the pizza, but she had said that it wasn't terrible. *A normal compliment for something that was gluten-free,* Drew had to admit. He heard the door open, then the exchange of voices.

"Andrew," Lexi greeted a moment later. She entered the kitchen quietly, Elena behind her.

Drew looked at her feet, noting she wasn't wearing shoes. Nor did she have her cane or wheelchair, which explained how she'd been so quiet. "Alexica," he replied, not taking the bait. He knew what she thought, knew how it seemed. *It didn't matter,* he told himself as he grabbed the towel and dried off his hands.

"The papers are in my room," he told his twin, motioning to the chair.

To his dismay, she followed him. "Why?" She questioned with a sigh. "Why do you insist upon doing this?"

"Bug off Lexi," Drew replied as he dug through his bag, grabbing the envelope. "Why don't you have a cane?" He handed her the envelope, waiting for her answer as he led the way back to the kitchen.

Not bothering to answer his question, Lexi sat down next to Elena at the counter. She watched as Drew picked up the dishrag again. "So, Elena - you're Tony's little sister?"

Elena smiled. "Little is a good word for it, but I choose to think he's tall and I am average sized. He is the older sibling, which I honestly like. It would be hard on my ego if he were younger than me and taller than me." She twisted on her chair so she faced Lexi, clearly not as upset about her interruption as Drew was.

He continued to scrub pizza sauce, this time off the pan. The sauce was stubborn when it had cooked onto something. It would be nice if he could just finish these dishes and figure out a way to kick Lexi out.

"Tell me about it." Lexi sent a glare Drew's way.

He gave her a shrug in reply. It wasn't like he could control his height. "I'm only two inches taller than you."

"And two minutes younger," Lexi told Elena. "That's the part I get to hold above him, he's the youngest of the family by a whole two minutes."

Elena laughed, her hand on her stomach as she did. "Gosh, I wish I could say that. I'm the youngest by six years. Two minutes seems a lot easier, you would have at least been in the same schools growing up. I was still in elementary school when Tony started high school. His first marriage happened while I was still in school. Were you in the same class, or did they separate you because you were twins?"

Drew sent Lexi a glance, telling her to say whatever she wanted. He'd go along with it, even if she wanted to tell Elena he'd been in so much trouble she'd had to be in the same class so she could keep an eye on him.

"We were always in the same class, I think." Lexi frowned for a moment. "We may have been in different preschool classes, but that's so long ago I can't remember. Our elementary school wasn't big enough to have more than one class per grade, so we were always together."

"And the rest of the grades?" Elena asked, leaning forward. "I nannied for twins, and they were fascinating. So much trouble when they wanted to be, but so much closer to each other than their other siblings. If I ever went to college, I'd make that my project, something about the psychology of twins."

"I had an accident before then," Lexi said softly. "I wasn't always able to be in school. We were always put in the same classes so Drew could keep me caught up on everything we were learning." She shot him a look he couldn't quite interpret, almost gratitude, but not quite.

Elena's eyes widened. "I'm so sorry, I didn't know. I did not mean to bring up anything painful, I just honestly had no idea. Natala talked so little about the two of you."

"That's great to know," Drew said as he pulled the plug on the sink, allowing the water to drain out. "I can use that against her in the future."

"I did not mean it for that purpose!" Elena exclaimed loudly, making both Drew and Lexi burst into laughter.

Lexi stood up, using the counter to help her. "I should get to Cameron's before he's wondering about me. I parked my car in his driveway and Daisy ran into the house, but I wanted to come grab these." She held up the envelopes, then looked at Elena.

"I like you. So please be careful with my brother. Drew is a player; he's never had the same girl more than a month. And he doesn't do serious relationships. You're related to my sister, and she seems to care about you. I don't want to lose her again." With that, she slipped out of the house as quietly as she came in.

Elena looked after her, seemingly frozen in place.

Drew shook his head and hung up the towel he'd been using. "She's trying to look out for you. Natala wasn't a big part of our lives for a handful of years. She lived in another state, didn't come home very often. Now that she's back, I think Lexi is afraid she will leave again."

Elena studied him, making Drew wonder what she was looking for. Trying to figure out if Lexi had been telling the truth? What had she thought about Lexi's rant? Or lecture, whatever his twin had considered it. She was trying to do the right thing; Drew couldn't fault her for that. He could be upset though. As Elena continued to study him, he watched her.

"I'm not worried," Elena said simply, looking out the glass door that led to the backyard. "We should go look at the stars. It's fascinating to be outside in the middle of the night, all the secrets the sky holds."

Drew glanced at the couch, disappointed that Pebbles hadn't come out. She seemed to prefer Elena to him. "Sure," he replied, turning off the lights in the house before he led Elena onto the porch.

Elena sat down on the stairs, then leaned back and looked up at the sky. "See all the stars? The big dipper is right over there"- She pointed as she spoke. "And the little dipper is right there. I'm still learning other constellations; those are the main two I know."

Drew sat down beside her. "Two is a great start to learning the constellations." The stars weren't what he was thinking about, but sure, he could go along with it.

He tried to focus more on the stars Elena was pointing to then the fact that she still smelled like raspberries. *Was it a perfume? A lotion?* He wondered.

"Most people don't stop to pay attention to them. They don't learn the constellations. They don't lay back and count the stars." Elena gave Drew a smile that seemed to light up her face. "They always talk about sunbathing, but the sun hurts. There's no peace laying on a towel in the middle of a crowded beach, hoping no one steps on you or throws sand at you." She looked up at the sky again.

"Moon bathing, that's what should be popular. The moonlight just gives everything in its path a magical shine, and it's so peaceful in the semi-darkness." She scooted down the steps till she was in the grass, then laid down.

Drew watched her from the stairs for a moment before joining her in the grass. The moonlight did seem to give her a magical shine, a glow almost. "You smell like raspberries and pizza."

Elena laughed, then covered her mouth with one of her hands. "That's a winning combination," she said, turning her head so she was looking Drew in the eyes. Hers seemed to sparkle with excitement and something else. Mischief maybe?

Drew's eyes dropped to her lips, and he found himself wondering if she'd taste as good as she smelled.

Elena's smile turned into a smirk as she scooted closer to him, till he could feel her breath on his face. "We are going to get grass stains on our clothes," she whispered.

"Too bad." Drew put his hand on her cheek, then kissed her. She tasted even better than she smelled. Like pizza and cranberry juice, a combination he didn't know would taste as perfect as it did.

Elena backed away a minute later, breathing heavily. Her cheeks were red as she met Drew's gaze, then giggled. "I feel like a teenager," she admitted.

Drew grinned. "So do I." He groaned as he saw his watch, then let his hand drop from her cheek. "To sound even more like a teenager, I have school tomorrow." He let himself fall back into the grass.

For some reason that made Elena giggle even more as she turned onto her side, facing him. "You should probably drive me home then. I mean, unless you're going to make me walk in the dark with a stalker on the loose. That might make our story turn into a horror film."

"We have a story?" Drew asked as he sat up, trying to pull the grass out of his hair.

"Of course, we have a story." Elena closed her eyes for a moment before sitting up. "Everyone that meets has a story. A short story, a long story, a comedy, a horror film..." She trailed off as she looked at his lips, a blush coming to her cheeks again.

"A romance. Whatever it may be, we have a story. We will see what it turns into." She stood up and flashed him a smile. "You're going to drive me home?"

"Yes." Drew gave up on the grass in his hair, figuring the cold shower he needed would get it out. He used the stairs to help himself stand up, then grabbed his keys and drove her home.

***

Drew was still thinking about that night as he got ready the next morning. He could still smell raspberries, still taste the pizza and cranberries. He hadn't said anything as he drove Elena home.

The only noise in the car had been Elena's directions, telling him how to get to her apartment. An apartment that had seemed a little sketchy to Drew, but she'd assured him that it had a good lock and she had taken self-defense classes.

Drew also had her number in his phone now, he remembered as he slipped his phone in his pants pocket. He grabbed the water tank from his coffee maker and filled it up, then pushed the button to start his coffee brewing. He'd insisted on having it, and her having his. Tony was out of the country right now. If anything happened, she needed someone she could call.

That was the angle Drew was using at least, trying to ignore the attraction that he had for her. He frowned as he pulled his travel mug – labeled "World's Best Teacher" - out of the coffee maker and attached the lid. Was it really being ignored if they had kissed? It seemed the attraction was mutual at least.

He grabbed a granola bar from the basket on the counter, then a second one. He tossed both into his bag on top of his laptop and zipped it up. As he did, he heard a scratching sound from the living room.

Slowly, Drew peeked his head over the counter. Pebbles had made her way out from under the couch and was playing with the toy he'd bought her. He grinned as he grabbed his keys, bag, and coffee. Maybe it was good for Pebbles that Drew worked so much, maybe she liked the house to herself.

Drew locked the house door behind him, then climbed into his car and clicked the button on his garage door opener. His phone buzzed in his pocket, something he ignored as he backed out of the driveway.

When he did check his phone – after setting up the classroom – he wasn't surprised to see the text was from his mom. *I'm making pizza meatloaf for dinner tonight; Lexi is making brownies before she goes to the chess club. Are you going to join us?*

Drew quickly sent back a text, confirming he'd be there just as the first bell rang. Students ran into his classroom.

"Good morning, everyone!" He greeted the seventh-grade class. "Today we are finishing our unit on graphs with one you should be familiar with." He looked around the classroom, noting some of the kids were watching him and some still seemed to be asleep.

"At least most of you were here last year, so you should remember the project you did on circle graphs! We are going to use this period to replicate that, but a little more complicated." His class groaned as Drew grinned, walking over to the whiteboard. He uncapped a marker and wrote on the top of the board as he spoke, "What is your favorite flavor of ice cream?"

He walked away from the board, picking up a small stack of papers. "Except this time there aren't just four answers." He shrugged. "I don't know how many answers there will be. Because instead of asking other people, we are going to answer as a class." He split the papers into eight groups, setting one on each of the front desks.

"Everyone needs to take a piece of paper, then pass it back. I want you to write down your favorite ice cream flavor." Drew sat back against his desk and watched the exchange of papers and furious writing. Two minutes later, he picked up his marker. "Pass them forward, please." He instructed.

Each of the students in the front desks read off the ice cream flavors that had been chosen. Drew wrote them on the board, adding tally marks when the favor was picked more than once.

"Alright class," Drew looked at his watch, "You now have twenty minutes to figure out percentages and make your circle graph. Remember, there are thirty people in our class today because George is out sick. So, thirty equals 100%."

Drew added that to the board, then sat down at his desk. "What are you waiting for?" He asked as he pulled out a notebook and pencil of his own. After all, if he wanted to find the correct answer and graph, he'd need to do the problem and graph himself.

***

"That was a lot of fun, Mr. Luna," Tenny told him as she bounced to his desk after the bell rang. "Can we do this every day? Ask a different question and make a graph about it? It's a whole lot more fun than figuring out what 'A' means."

Drew laughed. "I'm glad you enjoyed the activity Tenny, you did well with it and were fast to answer. Unfortunately, algebra is part of the curriculum I'm required to teach."

"Darn." Tenny's face fell. "I'm a lot better at the percentages."

"You know, I think you're better at algebra than you realize," Drew told her as he turned to another page in his notebook. "Like our problem today, what percentage of a hundred is chocolate? It's an unknown just like finding the letter 'A'. Giving it a label – like chocolate or strawberry – is a lot more fun than just calling it 'A'."

Tenny considered this, her foot rubbing against the floor. "I guess that makes sense." She looked at the clock, her eyes widening. "I need to get to my next class. Thanks Mr. Luna, I'll remember that!" She yelled as she ran down the hall.

Drew shook his head as he put the notebook back into his drawer and tidied up his desk. He'd always enjoyed math and had seen it as something bigger than just finding "A". If he could teach some of his students to think that way too, maybe they'd have a couple more people interested in entering a STEM field.

Or they could do all the money stuff Lexi did for Birdie's business. She claimed she was awful at math and hated it – that's why she wasn't a math teacher. Drew's arguments that science involved math had fallen upon deaf ears.

"Hey Mr. Luna!" Diego walked into the classroom and sat down at one of the desks. "Are we going to have any homework today? Because I'm already asking so many people about this grilled cheese thing, I don't have time for more homework."

Drew tried to hide his smile as he answered the sixth grader's question. "No, we will not have any homework this week. You'll have all that time to work on your chart. The question you chose is about grilled cheese?"

Diego sat up in his chair and grinned as other students came into the classroom. "Yeah! I'm trying to figure out what the best kind of cheese is to have on a grilled cheese sandwich."

"Sounds like you're having fun with your project." Drew looked around the classroom as students continued to trickle in.

"Anyone else having fun with their graph project?" He leaned back against his desk and listened as students told him the questions they were asking, and the places they'd asked. One girl's mother owned a hair salon, and she was asking everyone that came into the salon what their favorite pet was. As Drew listened, he tried not to let his students see how glad he was that they were learning math could be fun.

Chapter 6

Drew finished work, then hurried home. He was disappointed that Pebbles ran back under the couch as soon as he entered the living room. He set down his bag on a chair nearby, then lay down on his belly and looked under the couch.

"Pebbles, I promise I'm a good person." He frowned after he said that, wondering if that was really true. "I'm really good with dogs. I haven't met many cats yet, but you seem decent for a cat."

Surprisingly, Pebbles just stared at him. She was all the way against a wall, as far from Drew as she could be. Drew sighed and walked down the hall to his bedroom. He changed quickly, putting on a sweatshirt instead of the nice polo he'd been wearing.

After getting some of her food in a dish and setting it in front of the couch, Drew fished his keys out of the pocket. "I'm going to get some dinner myself," he told the cat. "I'll be back in a couple hours."

As he began walking to his childhood home, Drew wondered if Pebbles would play with her toy some more when he was out of the house. Maybe he should get her another toy or two to play with by herself, she seemed to like them.

"How was work today?" Connie asked a few minutes later as Drew let himself into the house that he'd grown up in.

Drew shrugged. "Normal. I'm doing the circle graph project, so it was interesting to hear how that's going." He looked around. "Where are Dad and Lexi?"

"Lexi has chess, it's Tuesday." Connie frowned as she glanced at the clock. "Although normally she would be back by now. I'm guessing she is just running late. And Dad is in the shower, some oil or something."

Drew sat down at the kitchen table and watched as his mom chopped some carrots. "One of the newbies?" He asked. His dad worked at an auto repair shop, and was often the one to train the new hires.

Connie frowned as she added the carrots to a bowl of lettuce, then grabbed a carton of strawberries. "I'm not actually sure," she replied. "He said something about slipping, so maybe it was on the floor? It certainly could have been a newbie's fault that it was on the floor."

Drew grinned. "Glad he's still fit enough he doesn't get hurt by slipping."

"Speaking of which," Connie glanced over to the door. "Your Dad and I are considering going on a cruise."

Drew sat back in his chair, considering that. He didn't know the last time his parents had been on vacation. Or the last time he or Lexi had been on vacation for that matter. It was probably before Lexi's accident – when they were just kids. His parents had never been on a cruise that he knew of. "That sounds like a great getaway for you and dad."

Connie gave him a tight smile. "It would be very nice," she admitted. "Your dad thinks we need it, but I'm not sure about Lexi."

Now Connie's continuous glancing at the door made sense. This was a conversation Drew wasn't supposed to tell Lexi about. "You haven't mentioned anything to her?" He asked, standing up.

"Not yet. We wanted to get some more solid plans in place first, maybe find a particular cruise and set up a time frame. I think going in winter would be nice, escaping the Wisconsin snowstorms and enjoying the sunbathing." Connie pulled out some shredded cheese and sprinkled it into her bowl.

Drew paced back and forth. "Maybe you should ask her about it. I assume you're worried about her being home alone?"

"She can't be." Connie cringed and glanced at the door again. "I don't mean to hurt her feelings at all, but I think she knows that. Even with her medications, she still has at least one morning a week she can't get out of bed. Daisy is a huge help for her and can do a lot – but not make her meals. And not call people on the phone to come help her."

Drew sighed. He hated that Lexi wasn't part of this conversation. It should be her decision. She may have some ideas for herself. Maybe she'd be willing to stay at his house. He voiced this to his mother, and she shook her head.

"It's not worth it right now. If we find one, we want to go on, then we can talk about it. Right now, it's just a possibility we are looking into." Connie set the bowl of salad on the table, then looked at her only son. "Why don't you go on vacation?"

Drew blinked. "Why would I go on vacation?" He asked in surprise. "You were the one going on vacation."

"You haven't left the state since you were nine. It would be good for you to travel some and see the country. Maybe then you'd settle down and get married. I want grandchildren, you know, and I'm not getting any younger."

"Mother." Drew's shoulders fell. "Natala literally just got married. You can bother her about grandchildren. And I'm a teacher. How much more settled can you get than that? I have a lot of kids already that I see almost every day. I can't just get up and take a vacation during the school year."

"I guess it wasn't a rational idea," Connie admitted. "I just think it would be nice for you."

"What would be nice for Drew?" Lexi asked as she wheeled into the house, Daisy by her side.

"Mom thinks that if I go on vacation, I'll give her grandchildren." Drew summarized; glad Lexi hadn't come home any earlier.

"Mother!" Lexi shrieked, echoing Drew's earlier statement. "You're just expecting him to go on vacation and meet someone there? Or knock some girl up?" She wrinkled her nose. "That's gross."

"First," Connie replied as she set a bowl of grapes on the table, "I did not mean that. I simply said that maybe if he went on vacation, he would be ready to settle down. Drew, don't you dare go knock anyone up."

Drew popped a grape into his mouth and grinned. "Why not?" He asked, watching as Connie turned red.

"What did I miss?" David asked as he came out of his bedroom. He noticed his wife's red face and looked at his children. "Who said what?"

"Mom told Drew to go have grandchildren. Then she told him not to knock up any girls, which completely contradicts the first statement." Lexi explained as she wheeled herself over to Daisy's dish.

Drew chuckled. He swore he could see the steam coming out of his mom's ears. This was why he liked family dinners; they were a whole lot more entertaining than eating alone.

***

"Andrew," Lexi called as he was walking down the driveway, ready to head back home.

He looked up at the sky, wishing she would disappear. Or that he'd imagined her appearance.

The only thing his brief moment of wishing accomplished was giving Lexi more time to wheel over to him. "What's bothering you?" She asked, looking him in the eye. "Was it Mom's comment? You haven't done anything wrong; you know."

"Wrong?" Drew asked with a frown.

"Moving out only a couple blocks from where you – we – grew up, going to college not far from here. There's nothing wrong with sticking close to home. You don't need to go see the world." Lexi bit her lip as her eyes widened. "Not that there's anything wrong with seeing the world either. Is that what's bothering you? Did Mom tap into some secret wish of yours to go on a trip or something?"

Drew shook his head, a bit amused by Lexi's theory. "To be honest, I've never thought about going on a vacation. I'm happy here. I like living close and having family dinners. There's something wrong with me, probably because I grew up with sisters. Too many females in the house, too many sentimental moments."

Lexi laughed. "You are just a social person," she replied. "I think you have to be, to teach all those different children each day. Think of how many different people you talk to on a daily basis."

"Too many to count," Drew said easily, glad the conversation had veered into less dangerous territory. "Especially when I go to a grocery store, or the pet store. I talk to people there."

Lexi rolled her eyes and backed away. "There's really nothing bothering you? I swear you seem off. It's something, I just don't know what." She narrowed her eyes as she looked at her twin. "There is something."

"There's nothing," Drew lied, wondering why he hadn't made a run for it when he had the chance. He felt like a child again, why could Lexi read him so well?

"I don't believe you. Is it something to do with Elena? Are you being stupid?"

"It's nothing to do with Elena. And I'm the smarter twin. I don't do stupid things. All my choices are highly calculated. They just aren't what you'd do if you had a choice." He looked at Lexi, her hands on the wheels of her wheelchair like she was some sort of superhero.

"I can't tell you Lexi, please don't ask. I promise it's not bad. It's just not my place to say anything."

His twin studied him for a moment more, before Drew watched her relax. "Fine, keep your secrets. I'm going to be at Cameron's tomorrow, but do me a favor and don't tell him I'm coming over please?"

Drew's eyebrows met as he frowned. "You are going to be at Cameron's house, but I should not tell him you will be there? Why am I even being told about this?"

"Just in case." Lexi shot him a grin as she turned around. "Don't worry about it, just if you see me don't say anything please. Have a good night!"

Drew watched her wheel back inside, wondering what she had planned for Cameron's house. *Why did she need to be there?* He sighed, shrugging it off as he began to walk. It wasn't really his problem.

He pulled his phone out of his pocket and opened the camera, curious to see if Pebbles had made her way out from under the couch. He noticed the bowl was empty, so she'd eaten her dinner at least. Moving the camera to look around the room, he didn't see Pebbles anywhere.

She must have gone back under the couch.

Drew looked at the grass as he walked, noting it was still brown. There could certainly still be some snow coming, and it would still be a couple weeks at least till the grass greened up. Then the flowers would start to pop up, and the grass would have to be mowed.

He walked up his driveway and looked at his own yard, realizing that mowing would probably need to happen sooner than later. The grass was long, and if there wasn't going to be any snow to cover it up it needed to be shorter.

Drew pulled out his keys and unlocked the door, then walked through the garage into his house. "Pebbles?" He called softly. "I'm home now." He set his keys on the counter so they would be ready when he needed them tomorrow morning. He grabbed a new thermos for his coffee and set that beside the coffee machine, because he hadn't washed the one that he'd used today.

Drew walked down the hall to his room. Now that he was home, he felt all the tiredness of the day come back to him.

A meow startled Drew as he walked into his bedroom. He backed up a bit when he noticed Pebbles laying in his laundry basket. "What are you doing there?" He asked the cat, taking slow steps towards her.

She gave another meow, this one a little quieter.

"Was I too loud when I came in?" Drew asked doubtfully. Pebbles had curled up into a ball. She was a lot smaller than he remembered. Or maybe she was just smaller than the dogs he normally fostered.

"Was it the sweatshirt?" Drew asked, running his hand through his hair slowly. He wasn't quite sure what to do. If he moved too much, would Pebbles leave? "You got used to the scent?"

He looked at the cat, who put her head back down and seemed to snuggle tighter into her ball. Drew shrugged, figuring he may as well continue as normal. Except he would have to put his laundry on the floor apparently, because now Pebbles had claimed the laundry basket.

***

She was still laying in the laundry basket when Drew woke up the next morning. "Good morning, Pebbles," he greeted the cat as he grabbed his clothes to go take a shower.

Drew showered quickly, then shaved and brushed his teeth. Lexi had always told him it was weird he brushed his teeth before he ate breakfast; but he wanted to get rid of morning breath as soon as he could.

He was disappointed to find the cat had moved when he came back into his room. It was a good opportunity to put his clothes into the laundry basket though, where they belonged.

Drew made his way to the kitchen, glancing at the living room as he passed. Pebbles wasn't visible, so she must have run back under the couch. *Maybe she'd had a bed under the couch at her old house,* Drew thought as he opened the fridge and pulled out his lunch. Maybe she wasn't just hiding from him as he'd originally thought. She was just used to being under the couch.

Or maybe she just doesn't like me, Drew thought with a laugh. He packed his lunch into his bag, then started his morning coffee. Taking a bagel out of the bag, he picked up a knife and cut the bagel in half. He popped both pieces in the toaster, then opened one of Pebble's food cans.

Drew put that into a bowl for the cat, then walked to the living room and set it down in front of her hiding spot. "Enjoy your breakfast," he told the couch, before grabbing his bagel from the toaster.

He sighed as the clock chimed. He was running late. Drew picked up his bag and coffee, then made his way out of the house. He took a bite of the bagel as he opened the car door, throwing his bag on the passenger seat and his coffee in the cup holder.

"I forgot my phone," Drew said aloud, his shoulders falling. He took another bite of his bagel as he got back out of the car. He unlocked the door and ran down the hall to his bedroom to grab the phone, which he hadn't even looked at this morning.

I don't have time to check it now, Drew thought to himself as he left the house again. This time he made it out of the driveway. Eating as he drove wasn't his favorite thing to do, but it was a lot better than being late. It did result in crumbs in his lap.

When Drew arrived at school, he brushed all the crumbs off his jeans that he could, then shrugged. None of the kids would care. After picking up his bag and taking a sip of coffee, he made his way into the school.

It was pretty small as far as schools went, but it seemed large to Drew. There had been an expansion built onto the school during his senior year, so it was a lot bigger than it had been when he'd been a student.

"Morning Drew!" Birdie called as he walked past her classroom, her red curls bouncing as she moved. She followed him across the hall to his classroom. "Question for you, have you ever considered tutoring?"

Drew narrowed his eyes as he set his bag on the chair. "That sounds like you are angling for something. Do you have a troubled child in your class that needs help? Or is it a student that you heard complaining about how difficult my class is?"

"Neither, actually." Birdie sighed as she leaned against one of the decks. "It's Sierra."

Drew took a sip of coffee, relishing the caffeine. Sierra was Birdie's daughter and business partner. "Sierra? She's in high school now, isn't she? She was always great with math when I had her."

Birdie raised her eyebrows. "That's what I thought. Geometry is getting the best of her. I don't know why, but she can't seem to pick it up. I know you don't teach high school, but maybe it would be less intimidating for her to have your help." She gave Drew a small smile. "That, and the fact that if she uses one of the tutors the high school recommends, her friends will find out."

"Good old high school." Drew shook his head. He'd heard about all the bullying that happened in high school, but he'd never experienced it. His high school years had been taken up with classes, then going home each night and making sure Lexi knew what she was doing in those classes. "As long as she is okay with it, I'd be happy to sit down with her sometime. I don't know how much help I'd be, but it's probably better if she gets frustrated with me for trying to help than her getting frustrated with you."

Birdie gave him a large smile this time, and he could see the relief in her eyes. "Thank you Drew," she said. "You'll make a great dad someday." With that statement, Birdie left his classroom a moment before his first student dashed in.

Chapter 7

"I can tell it is Wednesday. I have that midweek ick," Drew told Olivia, one of the sixth-grade aides as he met her in the hall that afternoon. "Felt like I was always running behind."

Olivia laughed. "I feel like I am running behind on sleep. That's what happens when you have a toddler, apparently." She rolled her eyes but her smile gave away her feelings.

"That's what happens when you have a toddler on your own. How much longer is your husband deployed?" Drew asked, opening the door for her.

Olivia stepped into the sunshine. "Two months," she replied. "He should be home a week before Ryan's birthday, which is cutting it a little close for my taste."

"Two months from now, school will be almost out," Drew commented, looking at the sun. "Then maybe we will finally be rid of some of these puddles."

"Or we will get more snow. Are you teaching summer school this year?" Olivia asked, pulling out her key fob and clicking a button.

"Not sure yet, maybe one of the months," Drew replied as he opened his car door, putting his bag inside the car. Their school did two different summer school sessions, and each lasted four weeks.

"The kids have more fun with summer classes. I think it's the shorter time period, they feel less stuck. I've heard a lot about your circle graph project, though. One of the kids is asking if a hot dog is a sandwich." Olivia pulled off the backpack she had been wearing and put it in the passenger seat of her van.

Drew frowned. "They are supposed to ask a poll question, one that has four choices. How are they getting four answers out of a yes or no question?"

Olivia laughed. "You've really never had a kid do that before? I thought someone would break the rules sooner. They do have four options– yes, no, I don't care, or I don't know."

Drew shrugged as he got into the driver's seat of his car. "Creative, I'll give them that. Sounds like a passion project. And no, I have never had a kid try that before. I guess I'll have to add that to the rules next year."

"You may want to," Olivia agreed. "Have a good night!"

"You too!" Drew called back before he closed his door and put on his seatbelt. He was going to make a quick stop at the pet store before going home. Pebbles seemed to be warming up some, and he hoped to find her another toy she could play with independently.

Speaking of which, Drew pulled his phone out of his pocket. He should see what Pebbles was doing at the moment, was she still under the couch? As he unlocked the phone screen, he was surprised to find he had a couple text messages from an unknown number.

Hey Drew, this is Elena. You gave me your number, but I didn't give you mine, so I figured I should introduce myself before I texted more.

Drew smiled, that sure sounded like Elena. He read the next message, then frowned.

I think I should take your advice and talk to the police. That guy is following me really closely now. I went to grab a coffee and he followed me into the shop. He's watching me right now. I'm trying to act normal, but this doesn't feel like a normal situation.

He looked at the time that message had been sent – 9:37am. That was almost seven hours ago.

Part of that might be that I don't have any kids with me. I'm so used to having munchkins follow me around. It's a lot more boring to drink my coffee and eat a pastry by myself, it feels weird. That's also part of the reason I'm texting you. Scrolling through social media would be my other option and that isn't my favorite thing to do.

For some reason, Drew wasn't surprised that Elena's texting style seemed to be long paragraphs. He looked out the windshield of his car, watching as the art teacher and her son walked by. Elena was a bubbly person; he'd gotten that from her pretty quickly. He could see how she would be a great nanny; the kids would probably love her. He glanced back at his phone, frowning as he saw the small bubble.

I'm standing up now and he's standing up too. I have a weird feeling about this. Elena had texted.

Drew stared at his phone, worry starting to rise up inside of him. He frowned even more when he noticed that had been the last text message that he had gotten from her. He glanced at the clock. She'd sent the message six hours ago. Why hadn't she sent anything else?

Drew clicked the call button, starting his car. Maybe she'd gotten busy with something and hadn't thought to update him. He sat impatiently in the seat, listening to the rings.

"Hello, this is Elena! I'm so glad you called, and so sorry I missed your call. Leave me a message or send me a text and I'll call you back as soon as I can!" Elena's voice rang in his ear, then he heard a beep.

"Hey Elena, it's Drew. You didn't say anything more so I just wanted to make sure you got back to your apartment or to wherever you were going fine. Talk later, bye." He hung up the phone, then looked at it for a moment.

Why hadn't she answered? Was she okay? Drew swallowed the doubts. She was probably just busy and hadn't heard her phone ring. Maybe she started a new job and couldn't answer her phone while she was working.

Drew took a breath, deciding to just let it be for now. *What else could he do?* He set his phone in the empty cup holder, then pulled out of the parking spot.

As he drove to the pet store, Drew tried to turn his thoughts to Pebbles. What other kinds of toys did they have for cats? Cats probably didn't play tug of war, so there wouldn't be any ropes.

***

Kenzie greeted Drew as soon as he walked into the pet store. "Hey Drew! I'm surprised you are back this soon, did you get a new foster already?"

"Nope, still the cat. She's not much of a fan of me, but she does like that one toy you showed me. Do you have other ones that she would play with on her own?" Drew asked, sticking his hands into his pockets. "I think she'd run away if I pulled out the mouse toy you gave me."

Kenzie laughed. "If you bring that one back, I can give you credit for it," she shrugged. "Or you can keep it until she is more used to you. I have a couple more for her to play with independently. How old is she? Is she an active cat?"

Drew lifted his shoulders in a shrug. "I'm guessing Pebbles is a couple of years old. She's not a kitten, but not elderly from what I can tell. I don't know how active she could be. She mostly hides from me. I've seen her dart away from me pretty fast, though. She plays with the other toy while I'm teaching, not when I'm home."

"Gotcha." Kenzie led him to the same aisle she'd shown him earlier in the week. "This one might be a good option. It's a laser pointer, but you can attach it to a wall or ceiling or window. There is a setting for you to be able to turn it on for her, or for it to turn on when it senses movement."

Drew took the box she handed him and studied it. The laser seemed to be shaped like a cat's head, something that he didn't think would impress Pebbles. "She would like this?" He asked Kenzie, the doubt clear in his voice.

"A lot of cats do." Kenzie laughed. "Dogs too. You could use it with your future canine fosters as well. They like to chase the laser, watch it, pounce on it, basically try to catch it. It would be a good way to get Pebble's brain working."

"I'll try it." Drew held the box, looking at the other items in the aisle. He saw a laser pointer that was handheld, but that wouldn't be something Pebbles could play with by herself. "Anything else? What's that playground thing?"

"Playground thing?" Kenzie frowned, then followed his pointed finger. "Oh, you mean the cat tower. They aren't cheap, but it would give her some more hiding spots." She looked at Drew. "Check with your shelter, see if they have any cat trees you could borrow. I'd guess they get donations and such. That way you can just give it back when you're finished."

"That doesn't make you a very good sales lady." Drew teased, making a mental note to call Gabi as soon as he got home. Maybe he could pick one up after school the next day. It would give Pebbles a new hiding spot for the weekend when he was home more.

Kenzie winked. "It's not all about the money. And I know you'll be back." She grinned. "If you have space and want more of a playground, you could get a tunnel. The cat tunnels have holes in the top of the tunnel too, a little different from the dog ones. And smaller of course."

"Collapsible like the one I got last year for the lab?" Drew asked. He'd put that tunnel in the backyard, and the black lab he'd been fostering had loved running through it. It was something Drew had sent with him when he went to his forever home.

"Exactly like that." Kenzie walked into a different aisle, Drew following. She handed Drew the tunnel.

"It's even the same fabric." Drew commented. "I'll try it. She might not care, but it's worth a shot. She could hide inside the thing too."

"Perfect! Anything else?"

"Should be good for now, I'll try out these. I'm guessing the laser thing has a manual or instructions to attach it to whatever?"

Kenzie led him to the checkout. "Absolutely. It involves screwing things into the wall or ceiling if you pick one of those routes." She scanned the laser she was talking about and added it to his bag. "I suggest the window route if you can do that, that one just uses a suction cup so there is no damage to your house."

Drew put in his card. "Thanks Kenzie, good to know."

"Anytime!" She ripped off the receipt and put that into the bag, then handed that to Drew. "See you next time!"

Drew nodded and opened the door with his back as he fished out the receipt, then put that into his wallet. He hoped Pebbles would enjoy at least one of the toys he'd gotten.

***

When Drew got home, he unpacked his work bag and made himself and Pebbles dinner. The cat was still enjoying her under the couch hideout. "I got you some new toys at the pet store," he said in the direction of the couch before he took a bite of chili.

Pebbles tentatively reached out her paw. It was if she was testing the air to make sure it was safe, Drew thought with amusement. He took another bite of chili as he watched the cat. She slowly made her way out of the couch, giving him a cautious look.

Pebbles continued to watch him while she ate. "How isn't that painful for you Pebbles?" Drew asked the cat. "Keeping your eyes up, on me, while your head is down eating your dinner. I'd hurt my eyes if I tried."

The cat didn't seem to care about his musings. Pebbles finished her dinner, then sat back and swished her tail, still watching him. She lifted one of her paws and began to lick it clean.

Drew finished his own dinner, then washed his dishes. He left Pebbles' bowl where it was, not wanting to scare her back into hiding. After he had finished that task, he grabbed the bag from the pet store and a pair of scissors.

He sat down on the floor in the living room, a couple yards between him and Pebbles. "I got two different things, which would you like to see first?" He set each one out on the ground in front of him, then waited to see what Pebbles would do.

She didn't seem to care, he realized. Pebbles was keeping her gaze carefully trained to him, the only time she had looked at either toy was when he had been setting it down. Drew shrugged. "I guess that means I pick."

He reached for the laser pointer cat head toy. The thing was small, which was a good thing. He opened the box, watching Pebbles. Her eyes were still on him, but now she had lay down.

"It does look like a cat's head." Drew commented, looking at Pebbles. "See? It's about the size of your head too." He set that down on the floor, and pulled out the other contents of the box. An instruction manual, a plastic piece, and a suction cup. "That's what we are going to use." He told Pebbles.

It only took a couple minutes for Drew to get the laser set up, but during that short time Pebbles made her disappearance. It was set up on the top of his sliding door, so now he was going to have to be sure not to open the door all the way.

Drew pushed the button on the top of the laser cat's head from the stepstool he was standing on. He blinked when he heard a scratching noise almost immediately. "Do you see it Pebbles?" He asked, watching as the red mark on the floor went in circles. It seemed repetitive, but maybe pets didn't notice that.

Pebbles peeked her head out from under the couch. She didn't notice as Drew got down from the step stool, didn't blink as he got closer to clean up the packaging. She was fully focused on the red dot.

Drew watched as she pounced on the laser, then watched as it moved away from her. "I'm glad you like the laser," he told the cat as he picked up the tunnel. Maybe he'd get that out for her tomorrow, save some of the new toys for a different time.

He remembered what Kenzie had said earlier about the cat tree and grabbed his phone. He dialed Gabi's number, then waited for her to pick up.

"They are still on vacation, if you are calling to see when Pebbles will be moving out." Gabi answered, sounding tired. "But I have a litter of puppies that will need fosters."

"Long day?" Drew asked, his eyebrows raised. "I don't want a whole litter of puppies; you remember how that went last time. And that's not what I'm calling about."

He heard Gabi take a deep breath, then let it out. "I do remember that. What are you calling about, then?"

"Does the shelter have any cat trees I can borrow? I went to the pet store today and saw a bunch of them with holes and spots to go in. Pebbles seems to like hiding, I thought she might like having one."

Gabi didn't reply.

"Are you still there? Did you fall asleep?" Drew asked her as he sat down on one of the barstools. He continued to watch Pebbles play with the laser, which she seemed to enjoy even more than her other toy.

"I'm just surprised," Gabi said finally. "I didn't think you'd get along with the cat. Um, cat trees." She sighed, "I think we have two in the back; you'd have to come check. If there's anything in the storage closet, you can certainly borrow it."

"I don't know if we are getting along. It's more like we tolerate each other," Drew replied. Pebbles had jumped onto the couch to watch the laser now. *Getting a higher vantage point,* he figured.

"Hey, whatever works. I need cat fosters too, maybe you should consider multiple pets. There are dog and cat pairs that I have to split up a lot of times because people only want a dog, or only want a cat."

Drew blinked, for some reason the thought of having a different cat seemed wrong. "I don't think cats are my thing, but I'll think about it. I'll come by after school to pick up a cat tree if you can tell whoever will be there."

"Sounds like a plan." Drew heard something in the background before Gabi came back to the phone. "I have to go. Bye."

The dial tone sounded before Drew could say goodbye. He shrugged, then took the phone to his room to put on the charger. He wasn't sure exactly where he would put the cat tree, but that sounded like a tomorrow problem.

Dew turned around, surprised to see Pebbles walk into the room. She made a graceful leap into the laundry basket, then curled into a ball and closed her eyes.

"I guess that's where you sleep now." Drew looked at the cat, wondering if she'd let him pet her. He seemed to be earning her trust, and didn't want to lose that. *I'll try in the morning, then if she gets scared, she will have some time to recover without me here.* Drew reasoned, then opened a drawer and got ready for bed.

Chapter 8

The next morning, Drew got up early. He didn't want to risk running late like he had yesterday, and Pebbles had been scratching at his door.

"I need to get a second litter box." Drew told the cat, rubbing his eyes as he opened the door for her to leave the room. Pebbles seemed to have decided his laundry basket was her bed.

After Drew showered and got ready for the day, he grabbed his phone and left the bedroom. Pebbles darted across the hallway, almost making him jump. "What are you doing?" He asked the calico, noticing the red dot a moment later. "You figured out how to turn on the laser, didn't you, girl?"

Pebbles didn't respond to him, instead she pounced on the laser. Drew chuckled as he walked into the kitchen and pulled out a carton of eggs. He grabbed a frying pan, sprayed it, then cracked two eggs into it. He made sure the burner was actually turned on, then moved on to making Pebbles' breakfast.

He opened a new can of food and put some of it into her little dish. "I wonder if you'll eat this somewhere else." Drew placed the bowl on the floor beside the counter. "Here Pebbles, your food is over here today. Do you want to eat?"

The cat glanced over to him, but didn't move away from the laser. Drew shrugged, figuring she'd find it later. He pulled a spatula out of a drawer and flipped his eggs over. A plate came out of the cabinet, and Drew poured himself a cup of orange juice.

When the eggs were finished cooking, Drew moved them from the frying pan to his plate, then took it over to the counter to sit down and eat. As he took a sip of his orange juice, Pebbles came running over. She sat down beside her dish and began to eat her breakfast.

The pair ate in silence, then Drew moved both his dishes and Pebbles' dish to the sink as Pebbles sat and licked her paws clean. Drew sat down on the floor beside the calico, and she eyed him as she finished licking her left paw clean.

Drew slowly reached out his hand, unsure if he should let her sniff it or not. That was what you did with dogs, but he swore he'd heard somewhere it wasn't right to do with cats.

Pebbles sat still, carefully watching Drew's hand as it moved closer to her. She didn't flinch as he began to pet her. "See? I knew we could be friends." Drew told the cat as he continued to pet her.

Pebbles' tail flicked as she stood up and walked away, deciding that she had had enough pets for the moment. Drew shrugged. He was surprised that she'd let him pet her at all. He stood up and packed his lunch for school. He still hadn't heard from Elena, and it was starting to worry him a little more.

He didn't know her that well, and had met her only a week ago. It didn't seem like she'd just ignore him after texting him. And the last text had not been reassuring at all.

Drew zipped up his bag and started his morning coffee, then pulled his phone out of his pocket and checked to see if he'd missed anything. One missed text from his mom. She instructed him to come for dinner that evening, something about Natala and Tony being back.

Drew frowned as he read that text again. *Why were they back already? Weren't they going to Italy?* It had only been a week, technically less than a week, since they'd gotten married.

He set that thought aside as he opened the text message thread from Elena and clicked the call button again. Drew leaned against the counter top as he held his phone to his ear with one hand, his other hand on his hip.

The phone rang and rang, then, "Hello, this is Elena! I'm so glad you called, and so sorry I missed your call. Leave me a message or send me a text and I'll call you back as soon as I can!"

He shook his head and hung up, not sure what he'd say if he left another message. Drew glanced at the clock. He had ten minutes till he needed to leave. He opened the web browser app and typed "missing persons" into the search engine.

Ten minutes later, after a lot of scrolling and reading through various articles, Drew figured there was really nothing he could do at this point. Elena was an adult, and she'd only been "missing" for twenty hours.

He grabbed his bag and coffee. Elena could just be hiding in her apartment for that matter, or have her phone turned off. Or have lost her phone, any simple explanation like that. "Bye Pebbles," he called to the cat as he walked into the garage.

His mom had said that Natala and Tony would be home tonight. If he hadn't heard anything by then he'd talk to Tony. Elena's brother may have heard from her, and maybe he knew more about her stalker then he'd told her.

Drew started his car and began his drive to school, trying not to think about Elena. Something that was very difficult for some reason. Even before the mysterious text messages. He'd never had problems thinking too much about a girl before, it was usually easy to put whoever he was seeing out of his mind while he was working or with family. With Elena, that was harder. Maybe because she wasn't really a girl he was seeing. There'd been one kiss.

Drew put on his blinker and came to a stop at the stop sign. Even if he wanted it to, one kiss did not make it a relationship. And at the moment, he had no clue where Elena was or what she was doing. For all he knew she was on a date or something like that.

***

Drew found that his classes were getting even more excited about the project the more they worked on it. His first sixth-grade class had set a contest between them on who could ask the most people their question, and one of the children had already made it to a hundred.

It was one of the fun parts of teaching, watching the kids get into an assignment.

They may get a little less excited when they had to do the math and turn their numbers into percentages, then make those into a graph, but at the moment he was glad they were enjoying it. It made for an easier school day when the kids were happy.

Drew packed up his bag at the end of the day, then pulled out his phone. Connie had texted him again, asking him to run to the grocery store for some strawberries. He sent a thumbs up back, then noticed he had one missed call from Elena.

He pulled up his voicemail, noticing he had a thirty second one from Elena. He clicked play, then clicked the speaker so he could hear it a little louder. "Hey Drew, I'm fine. I think I lost him now. I'm in some little town at a hotel."

Drew stared at the phone. *That was it?* Elena had not sounded like her bubbly self, and the message seemed almost like it had been cut off. He wished she would have mentioned what little town she was in, that would have made him feel better.

Worry nagged as he slipped the phone back into his pocket and grabbed his bag and coffee, then made his way out of the classroom. He had two errands to run now, the shelter and the grocery store. Of course, they were on opposite ends of town, so he'd be rushing to make it home in time for dinner.

Drew decided to go to the grocery store first, because that would be a quicker stop. He walked through the sliding doors and caught sight of the tulips. The local grocery store always sold tulips this time of the year, they were usually good quality and only $7 for a bouquet.

He picked up a basket from the entrance, then made his way to the tulip display. He looked at the different bundles, before selecting two that hadn't completely opened yet.

"Natala," he said aloud, remembering that his older sister would be present at dinner as well. He selected another bouquet and added that to the first two. Technically, Lexi was also older than him; but he preferred to think of them as being the same age. Two minutes didn't make that much of a difference, just gave Lexi some bragging rights.

Drew grabbed two cartons of strawberries, not paying too much attention to them. They were red, so they had to be decent. He walked toward the checkout counter, then noticed the pet aisle. *I've only got one can left of food for Pebbles,* he thought as he walked into the aisle. It took him only a moment to find the brand he'd been feeding the cat.

He looked at the cans, then noticed the box that was above them. "Forty cans," he read, thinking about it for a moment. He grabbed the box, then made his way to one of the self-checkouts. He scanned his purchases, making sure the flowers didn't get crushed.

Getting everything into the car was more difficult than he wished, because the front seat wasn't empty for the flowers. He wasn't sure how much room the cat tree would take up, and he might need to put the backseat down to fit it into his car.

Drew set the cat food on the floor of the passenger seat, then put his work bag beside it. He put the strawberries on top of that and covered them with a blanket so the sun wouldn't get to them. Then he sat the flowers carefully on the seat, hoping they would be safe there.

The drive to the shelter took fifteen minutes. "Hey Esther," he greeted the receptionist as he walked inside the building. "Gabi said there is a cat tree here somewhere that I can borrow."

Esther smiled at him. "You're warming up to the cat?" She asked as she glanced at her desk, likely looking for a sticky note. Esther's desk was always full of various sticky notes.

"I think she's warming up to me. Your sweatshirt suggestion really did the trick, maybe a little more than you intended. She's taken to sleeping in my laundry basket now," Drew told Esther, watching as she held up a purple sticky note in victory.

Esther laughed. "That's great!" She exclaimed. "That means she's comfortable with you." She stood up and opened the door to the back room. "The cat tree should be in here..." She trailed off as she looked around.

Drew followed her into the back room, which was really a staff room. Or was supposed to be, it doubled as a storage room. "That one?" He asked, pointing to a large pink tower.

"That looks about right!" Esther moved back. "I'll let you grab it. I don't think it will be that heavy, but these old arms aren't as strong as they used to be."

"You're in great shape Esther." Drew replied as he made his way to the cat tree. "You can handle squirming animals. That takes a different kind of strength many people don't possess. Myself included, give me something heavy over something squirming any day." He picked up the cat tree, noting it really wasn't that heavy. It should fit into the car, so that was a good sign.

Esther laughed again as she held the door open for him, then walked ahead of him to open the front door for him. "It's just a different learning process," she replied, walking ahead of Drew to his car. "Which door?"

"Either of the back doors. I think this will fit on the backseat. Or I'm hoping that it will, I don't have another thought." Drew waited for Esther to open the door, then maneuvered the cat tree inside. It did fit – but he wouldn't be able to see out the back too easily as he drove.

"Thanks Esther. You don't happen to have an extra litter box by chance, do you?"

Esther laughed as she led the way back to the building. "It's an animal shelter. We have plenty of litter boxes. I can get you another one." She walked into the back room again, this time coming back a moment later. "Here you go. You still have some litter right?"

Drew thought about the bag that was sitting in his garage. The one that Gabi had brought with Pebbles. "Yeah, plenty," he replied, taking the empty litter box she offered. "Thank you again."

"Anytime!" Esther replied with a big smile as she sat back down at her desk. "Enjoy the little kitty."

"I will," Drew replied, opening the door to go outside. He was almost disappointed that Elena didn't run into him this time. That would have answered all his questions, or at least most of them.

Drew tossed the litter box in the back seat, then checked his watch. He was supposed to be at Connie's now, so there was no time to drive to Elena's apartment and check to see if she was there. *Maybe after I leave Mom's,* he thought as he started the car.

***

Drew pulled into the driveway, then grabbed the strawberries and the flowers. He let himself into the house. "Anyone home?" He called.

"Hey Drew," Connie said from the kitchen. "Dad, Natala, and Tony are in the backyard. Lexi is in her room, trying to relax. Did you bring strawberries?"

"I did," Drew replied, setting them down on the counter as Connie dried her hands on a towel. "I also got these for you." He handed her one of the tulip bouquets.

"Oh Drew, that's so sweet of you." Connie gave her son a hug then opened one of the cabinets. "Can you get a vase down for me?"

Drew set the other two bouquets on the counter, then pulled out two vases from the cabinet. He filled each with water, then set his mother's flowers into one of them and left it on the counter. He added one of the other bouquets to the second vase, then walked down the hall to Lexi's room.

"Come in," Lexi called softly when Drew knocked. He opened the door slowly, noting the room was dark and Daisy was lying on Lexi's lap. "Over-stimulated or more?" He asked, closing the door so the room stayed dark.

Lexi sighed. "Just overstimulated. I'm trying to decompress before I interact with too many people again."

"Sorry Lexi." Drew held out the vase of flowers for her. "I brought you some flowers. Where would you like me to put them?"

Lexi's face lit up when she smiled. "Thank you Drew." She glanced over at her desk. "You can move some things on the desk and put them there. The receipts get put into that green plastic box."

Drew piled the receipts into the box mentioned carefully, then set the vase down on the desk where Lexi could see it. He sat down on the bed and pet Daisy. "Are you being a good girl, helping Lexi?"

"Of course she is." Lexi answered for the dog, smiling at her. "How's it going with the cat?"

Drew raised one shoulder in a shrug. "Pretty well, I guess. She's warming up to me. I got this laser thing for her yesterday and she is really enjoying that." His eyebrows met as he frowned. "And she has chosen my laundry basket as her bed."

Lexi giggled. "Poor Drew. He lost his laundry basket. Life will never be the same." She teased.

Drew shook his head. "Never," he replied, giving Daisy another pet. "Why are Natala and Tony home?" He asked. "I thought they were going to Italy."

"Oh, they didn't make their flight." Lexi frowned. "Or the flight didn't go. I don't know the plane terms. Bad weather or something. They wouldn't have been able to fly there for three more days, so they found a hotel in the Dells instead. I guess they could cancel all their reservations in Italy without a problem."

"Makes sense, I guess. Mom was telling me to go on vacation. Maybe I should make a trip to the Dells." Wisconsin Dells was a city about an hour away from their small town. It was the waterpark capital of America, and a place they had gone to as a family once a year when they were kids.

The entire family had gone for the first ten years. That last year, Lexi had a difficult time with the chlorine smell and the noise of the water parks. After that, it had just been him, his dad, and Natala.

"You should go talk to them; they may have a good recommendation on where to visit. I'll be out in a couple more minutes."

Drew stood up, brushing the comforter on Lexi's bed back into place. "Stay as long as you need to. I can make a plate for you if you need it," he told her.

Lexi gave him a smile. "Thanks Drew. And thanks for the flowers, I appreciate them every time."

Drew left Lexi's room, taking care to shut the door very quietly behind him. As he made his way to the backyard, he grabbed the third bouquet.

"Hey Drew!" David lifted his beer in greeting. He was sitting on a lawn chair, Tony on another beside him. Natala was sitting on her husband's lap.

"Hey," Drew replied, handing the tulips to Natala. "Happy spring."

Natala smiled at him, taking the flowers and lifting them to her nose. "Thank you Drew." She turned to her husband. "When Drew was younger, he always got us tulips when they came to stores in the spring. He'd save his lawn mowing money and buy a bouquet, then split it between Mom, Lexi and I."

Drew shrugged as he pulled over another lawn chair. "I make a little more now than I did when I mowed lawns." He turned to Tony. "I heard you went to the Dells instead of Italy for your honeymoon."

"We did," Tony replied, looking at Natala. "It was very much a different experience than Italy. I had never been to the Wisconsin Dells, so it was very cool to see."

Before Drew could reply, Connie called them all in for dinner. Drew's phone buzzed, and he stopped to check it before he joined the others inside. It was Elena. She'd sent a text message. Drew felt his heart pounding as he read that message. *He found me.*

Chapter 9

Drew stared at his phone, not really seeing it anymore. He didn't know how to reply to that message, nor did he know what to do in this situation. Elena was in a small little town; how would he tell the police that? It wasn't helpful, she hadn't given him the name of the town. He had no clue where she was.

"Drew?"

Drew looked up from his phone, Tony walking towards him. "I was sent to come see what's taking you so long."

"Your sister," Drew replied, figuring now was as good a time as ever to catch Tony up, maybe he knew what small little town she was in.

"Elena?" Tony asked, crossing his arms over his chest.

Drew tried to ignore the panic welling up inside him. He was in control, he had to be the strong one. It had always been that way; he took care of his mom when his dad worked late. He took care of his twin; he comforted her when she had hard days.

The girls... the girls were supposed to be the fun part. The easy part, but this didn't feel fun or easy.

"Elena ran into me twice this week," Drew explained. "Literally ran into me, looked like she was terrified. She said she had a stalker. I gave her my number because I thought you were in Italy and she needed someone to call if anything happened."

Tony frowned. "Her stalker disappeared when she moved to Italy."

Drew shrugged, holding out his phone for Tony to read. "He came back. She just didn't want you to know. You were on your honeymoon, she wanted you to enjoy that."

Tony took the phone and read the messages, his frown deepening. "The last one is ominous."

"She left a voicemail before that one, saying that she'd found a small town not too far away to stay in. But no mention of the town name or anything that could tell me where she is." Drew glanced at the last message again. It had been sent three minutes ago now, maybe she still had her phone and was waiting to reply.

He typed out a text quickly and sent it to her, asking where she was and if she was okay.

"Tony, Drew, come on! Food is going to get cold!" Natala called from the porch.

Tony looked at Drew. "Don't say anything at dinner," He advised. "It's not worth worrying everyone."

Drew nodded, following Tony to the dinner table. If his phone buzzed at all he'd be looking at it, no matter how rude that may be to do at the dinner table.

***

When dinner was finished, dessert had been presented and eaten, and the dishes were washed, Tony turned to Drew. "Hey Drew, I wouldn't mind a tour of your house. Natala was telling me you bought one just a few blocks from here?"

"Yep. It's about a five-minute walk, three-minute drive," Drew replied, pulling his keys out of his pocket. "I can give you the tour." He figured this was Tony's way of getting them somewhere they could speak freely.

"Enjoy the time with your parents," Tony said to his wife, giving her a wink. He followed Drew outside.

Drew put the cat food and his bag in the backseat of the car, allowing Tony room to sit in the passenger seat. He pulled out of the driveway. "Have you heard from her at all since you got back?"

Tony shook his head as he looked out the car window. "Nothing, but she doesn't know I'm back yet. We don't talk that often ordinarily; she was always busy with nannying. And I was busy traveling for work."

Drew nodded, pretending to understand. He didn't really; he had two sisters and very different relationships with both. He and Lexi were best friends. They had the twin bond and texted all the time. On the other hand, he didn't even have Natala's phone number.

Drew pulled into his driveway and hit the button to open the garage door. "Have you tried texting her at all?" He asked as he parked the car.

"I sent a message right before we started eating, but nothing before that. Haven't gotten a reply but no surprise there." Tony got out of the car. "The stalker came back? Did she say anything about what he looked like? She's never told me that much; I've never seen him myself."

Drew opened the door and led the way into the house. "Nothing about that. I didn't see him at all either, she'd just run into me red-faced and worried. I know less than you do I'd expect." He glanced into the living room, not seeing Pebbles.

"She's in a small town." Tony looked around Drew's house. "How many small towns are around here?"

Drew gave a snort. "Most of Wisconsin is small towns." He replied as he peeked under the couch. Sure enough, Pebbles was back in her original hiding spot. Drew felt a small wave of relief that she was fine, something that surprised him.

"There are a lot of them around here." Drew pulled up his voicemail, then played the one from Elena again.

"Hey Drew, I'm fine. I think I lost him now, I'm in some little town at a hotel because I didn't want him to find my apartment."

"A hotel!" Tony snapped his fingers. "We could call hotels to see if they have anyone with her name registered there. But I think she would tell them not to let anyone know she was there."

"If I had a stalker I would," Drew replied. He grabbed Pebbles' empty dish and pulled the can of cat food out of the fridge, then spooned some into the bowl. He set it back down beside the counter so she could eat it whenever she wanted to.

"I was going to try her apartment, see if there was anyone there who knew where she went." Drew glanced at Tony, wondering how protective he was of his sister. Would he care that Drew knew where Elena's apartment was?

"Good idea. I have a key to her apartment. Maybe she left her reservation for the hotel on her laptop or something."

The pair got back into Drew's car, then made the drive to Elena's apartment. Tony was on his phone the entire car ride, looking up the closest hotels. "There are so many, it would take forever to call each one of them."

Drew nodded as he pulled into a parking spot. "Sounds about right. Some are not great, but Elena may not know that so we can't knock them off the possibility list."

They walked into the apartment building and took the elevator to the third floor. When Drew got to Elena's apartment, he froze. The door was already open.

"Elena?" He called, walking inside without thinking about Tony. *Why was the door open? If Elena was at a hotel, who was inside her apartment?*

He didn't know the layout of the apartment, where to look, or even what he was looking for. All he knew was that there was a reason that door had to be open, and he had to find it.

Drew glanced around the kitchen, seeing a notebook, but nothing else. He didn't bother to read it. If someone was in the apartment, he wanted to find them. They should know where Elena was.

He opened the first door he saw, which turned out to be the bathroom. Nothing was out of place there, but he noted the raspberry smell. If it was a strong smell, didn't that mean Elena had been here recently?

Drew left the bathroom and opened the next door, coming face to face with a stack of towels. He stepped back and did a quick glance up and down the closet. Nothing was odd or would help him in any way. He closed that door, turning around and glancing around the apartment.

There had to be another door. She had to have a bedroom at least. A fire escape should be somewhere. Where was that? Or was that just a thing in books and movies?

Tony was sitting at the counter reading the notebook, something that escaped Drew's notice completely as he saw the third door.

Drew almost ran over to it, flinging it open. It seemed to be the bedroom, as he'd suspected.

What he hadn't predicted was what was laying on top of the bed – a ghostly white Elena.

"Elena," he breathed, running over to the bed and gathering her into his arms. Relief bubbled up inside him. He felt like he could breathe for the first time that night.

He heard footsteps pounding, and a moment Tony was in the doorway. "Elena Marie Calo, you scared the heck out of me."

Elena looked at him slowly, her voice emotionless when she said, "You are supposed to be in Italy."

Drew frowned. That didn't sound like Elena at all. Her hands were still, something else he found odd. Elena always talked with her hands. "Are you okay? What happened?" He asked her, sitting down on the bed. He grasped her hands in his, wishing her skin wasn't as pale as it was.

Elena just shook her head, closing her eyes. Tears leaked out silently, and she squeezed Drew's hands.

Tony put his hand on Elena's forehead, then backed away. "Elena, what happened? Did he do something to you? If I ever find him..." He held up the notebook.

"You wrote it all down in here. This can be taken to the police. They should do something." He flipped to a page and showed it to Elena. "Here you wrote down a physical description of the man. That should give them something to work with."

"It doesn't matter," Elena said, taking one of her hands from Drew's and covering her face.

"It doesn't matter?" Tony stared at his sister. "Elena, you've been avoiding this guy since you were sixteen, since you were still a child. And now you say it doesn't matter?"

Elena shook her head. "He wasn't stalking me." No emotions were present in her voice, it was as if she was reciting something.

"He wasn't stalking you?" Drew asked, confused. Elena didn't seem upset necessarily, just withdrawn. In a way it was more worrying than if she'd been upset. "You told me he was. You texted that he was following you."

Elena blinked, her hand starting to trace the floral pattern on her comforter. She still hadn't looked at either Drew or Tony. "He was following me. But he wasn't a stalker, he was a private investigator."

"Why was a private investigator following you?" Tony was the one who seemed pale now. "Elena, did you do something?"

At that statement, a bit of color returned to Elena's face. "Did I do something? I was born, apparently that's what I did." She gripped Drew's hand tightly.

He wasn't sure if she was conscious of the fact, but he didn't mind. If it helped Elena, that was what he was here for.

"Why was a private investigator following you, Elena?" Drew asked her softly.

"My father hired him," Elena answered, her face losing the color it had regained. "My biological father." She glanced over at Tony.

"Did you know?" She asked. "Did you know that the man I called my father wasn't my biological father? Did you know that he threatened my biological father, told him he was never to reveal the truth?"

Tony stood, almost frozen. "What?"

Elena shrugged. She was trying to portray carelessness, Drew suspected, but he could feel her heart racing.

"That's why he started following me when I was sixteen. The threat was over, he could see how I was doing. The private investigator told me he was to watch over me until I turned eighteen, then tell me the truth." She looked at Tony. "But when I turned eighteen, I left."

"How do you know he was telling the truth?" Drew asked. It sounded a little far-fetched, like a story the man may have made up to explain why he was stalking Elena.

She nodded to the dresser. "It's all there." She gave a small laugh. "My birth certificate names Tenzel White as my father. Emails he exchanged with, or rather got from, Dario Calo. His death certificate and will, because that's the other part of it. My biological father died last year. I never got a chance to meet him. The private investigator wasn't even getting paid anymore, he just wanted me to have my inheritance."

Tony picked up the bundle, looking through the things inside it.

Drew watched, not sure what he was seeing. Tony wore a frown, but that could have come from anything.

After a moment, Tony set the bundle back down. "That's what it says," he admitted, eyeing Elena.

The room was silent for a moment, it seemed not one of the three knew what to say next. Tony ran his hand through his hair. He looked at Drew and Elena, who were still holding hands and sitting very close together.

His eyes narrowed. "Maybe you should add some space there," he said, as if noticing for the first time Elena "running into" Drew wasn't completely innocent.

"More important things are happening right now," Elena told her brother, her skin seeming to gain a little more of its color. Drew was glad to see it. It seemed anger could bring Elena back to reality.

"We have time to figure things out." Tony glanced at the papers as if they were an intrusion. "And we need to talk to Mom. Right now, maybe you should move away a bit. Trauma bonds aren't the best relationship starter."

Elena's eyes widened; her hand squeezing Drew's even tighter. "Trauma bonds? I'm not traumatized. I'm shocked, shaken, but not traumatized."

"Whatever it is. I've heard plenty of stories, Elena. Stories that you haven't heard yet. He jumps from girl to girl all the time. You'll just be one of many. Heck, in the two years since I met Natala, I can name at least a dozen girls he's been out with. Drew has never had a serious relationship. What makes you think this one is going to be any different?"

Elena smiled. "Because I'm a lot smarter than you give me credit for." She untangled her hand from Drew's and stood up. As she used her hands to pull her skirt down, Drew realized he missed her hand in his.

"I've grown up Antonio," Elena told him, sparks accompanying her words. "You got married when I was twelve, still a child. I've seen you maybe four days a year since then, we don't talk all that much. You don't know me as well as you think you do."

"I'm not a child anymore, I'm almost twenty-four. I've dated before, and I know how to read people." Elena turned to Drew and gave him a shy smile. "Andrew," she started, using his full name. The only people who used his full name were Lexi or his mother, when they were upset with him. Somehow, it sounded perfect when it came out of Elena's mouth.

"He puts up a great facade, tries to make people think he doesn't care about the women he dates. He can't spend too long with any one girl, because then he may start to have feelings for them and he doesn't want that." Elena sighed.

"What no one seems to see, what he doesn't want anyone to see, is that he does care. He cares deeply about people, and he already has enough people in his life to take care of."

She shrugged one shoulder. "I'm sure Lexi could pick a petty argument or something almost silly, but he's never hurt her. Drew spent a lot of his school years taking care of Lexi, teaching her and making sure she didn't fall behind. He's never been in a serious relationship because he already has enough people in his life to take care of, along with the foster animals and the children he teaches."

Drew stared at her in shock, trying to figure out how she knew all that. No one knew that, even Lexi hadn't realized the true reason he didn't do serious relationships. She figured he was just having fun, that he'd settle down eventually.

There was a soft clapping coming from the bedroom doorway, and all three turned to see Natala in the doorway. "The door was open. The tracking app said Tony was here." She gave a small shrug with her explanation.

"Well said Elena," Natala told the girl as she walked over to her husband. "As I recall, it's not that far off from what you said to me after Italy."

Tony looked down at Natala, not saying anything.

Natala slipped her arm around his waist as she smiled at Drew and Elena. "That's his way of saying he remembers. He has no argument because it's true." She looked directly at Drew. "Lexi talked to me, explained her concerns about you and Elena. I wasn't sure what to think, that's why I came to find you. Now," she gave a small laugh, "I think you'll be fine."

"Never asked for your blessing Nat," Drew told her as he got up from the bed. "But thank you."

Natala grinned. "No problem," she replied, leading her husband out of the room.

Drew turned to Elena, suddenly unsure what to say.

Elena giggled, seemingly having the same problem. "How is Pebbles?" She asked, walking closer to him.

"She's great. Decided my laundry basket is her new bed." Drew looked into Elena's eyes, fighting the urge to kiss her. She was beautiful.

"Do you want to go see her?" He glanced at the bed. "Having a chaperone might not be a bad idea."

Elena raised an eyebrow. "I have no objections. But I'm not sure how much of a chaperone a feline would be."

Chapter 10

It turned out that a feline was a good chaperone. At least a cat with a laser, because she was very entertaining. Pebbles was playing with it when they walked into the house. Elena sat down on one of the bar stools to watch her antics.

"Get it, Pebbles!" Elena cheered with a giggle. The cat stopped for a moment and looked at Elena, then pounced on the red dot.

Drew glanced below to Pebbles' food dish, glad to see it was empty. He moved it to the counter. "Did you eat anything for dinner?" He asked Elena, remembering how pale she had been and the timing of her text.

Elena looked over her shoulder at him and blinked. "I guess I didn't," she replied, then frowned. "I didn't eat anything for lunch either. That's strange, I like to eat. Why didn't I eat?"

"Because you were on edge and not focused on food," Drew replied, opening his fridge. He dug around for a moment, then pulled out a container of taco meat. He took the sour cream, salsa, shredded cheese, and lettuce head out of the fridge.

"What's that package?" Elena asked, pointing to the tunnel that Drew had left beside the stove.

"It's a tunnel for Pebbles, I haven't gotten it out yet to see if she likes it." Drew set the ingredients on the counter, then handed the tunnel to Elena. "You can get it out for her."

Elena did just that as Drew heated up some meat. He grabbed a bag of tortilla chips and put that on the bottom of a bowl, then shredded some lettuce before adding that meat on top. Salas and sour cream went next, then he sprinkled on some cheese. After grabbing a spoon, he handed it to Elena. "Your dinner."

Elena grinned at him and left the tunnel on the floor as she stood up and sat down at the counter. "Thank you very much. It looks so pretty, and it smells delicious. I love tacos, it had been forever since I had one." She inhaled the scent of the bowl, then took a bite.

Drew chuckled. "Just don't tell my sisters it was beautiful. That sounds like something I'd never live down." He picked up the tunnel from the floor and untied the last two ties that kept the tunnel compacted. The tunnel sprang open, the sound making Pebbles jump.

The cat gave him a scolding look.

"It's for you Pebbles," Drew explained, setting it down on the floor. "See? It's a tunnel, you can crawl through it."

Pebbles looked from him to the laser, as if saying *why would I want a tunnel when I have this laser?*

Elena laughed, then covered her mouth with her hand. She finished the bite that was in her mouth before she spoke. "I'm sorry, I couldn't help it. She has a little bit of an attitude to her. Right Pebbles? You aren't afraid to put Drew in his place."

"Great, I needed another female to do that in my life." Drew muttered under his breath. He glanced at Elena, who seemed to be distracted with her taco bowl.

"Your laser is going to die at some point, Pebbles," he told the cat, standing up. He picked up the tunnel and moved it so it was against a wall, near the couch. "It will be here when you want it."

"What was the big pink thing in the back of your car?" Elena asked between bites of her dinner. "It looked very fuzzy. Which is weird, because I wouldn't have thought you were a person who likes fuzzy decorations. Or the person who would like pink."

Drew groaned when he remembered the cat tree. "That's still in the car. It's a cat tree for Pebbles, with boxes and whatever for her to hide in and a perch to sit on. I got it from the shelter, they picked the pink. I have to get that inside somehow, without letting Pebbles out."

Elena giggled and scraped her bowl with her spoon. She finished that bite, then stood up. "I can help. I'm great at holding doors, and I'll keep my eyes peeped in case Pebbles decides to investigate."

"That would actually be great." Drew took her bowl from the counter and rinsed it out, leaving it in the sink. He followed Elena out to the garage and struggled to get the cat tree out of his car. It didn't help that his work bag and a large box of cat food were in the way.

"Here," Elena laughed as she grabbed the bag off the cat tree. "I'll take that, it's probably safer for me to hold it. Do you want me to grab the cat food too?"

Drew tried to adjust his grip on the cat tree. It wasn't that heavy, but it was quite awkward. "You don't have to, but if you can, feel free."

Elena picked the box up easily, then ran to the door and opened it for Drew to bring the cat tree into the house. "Nannying is actually a great workout," she informed him as she closed the door. Elena set the cat food and bag on the counter, watching as Drew set the cat tree down in the middle of the living room.

"That's a statement piece for sure. It really adds some color to the room, like a bright color." Elena looked at it doubtfully. "I'm not sure that's the best place for it."

Drew sighed as he looked around the living room. He had a couch, two chairs, and a coffee table. There was a plant or two and a shelf, but that was pretty much all that was in his living room. Besides the new cat toys, litter box, cat tree, and laser that pointed into the room. "I'm not sure where the best place for it is."

Elena frowned for a moment. "You should move the litter box. It's too," She scrunched her nose, "Weird in the living room. Put it in like a closet or the bathroom, somewhere a bit more hidden from guests. Then you could move the toys over there, and put the cat tree beside the couch; against the wall."

"That would work." Drew picked up the litter box and carried it to the master bathroom. He would get the new one set up in a closet or something like Elena had suggested, but for now this would suffice.

Drew got back to the living room to find Elena had already moved the toys, and one of the plants so it fit with the toys.

"Have you ever looked up if these plants are safe for cats?" She asked as she inspected the pot. "I know some plants are bad for cats, if they eat them or something. I have no clue what those plants are."

Drew picked up the cat tree and moved it to the corner of the room, noting it did fit pretty well there. The pink wouldn't have been his color choice. Hopefully, Pebbles appreciated it. "I haven't looked up the plants. But when I got them, I let the place I bought them know I foster dogs. They have to be somewhat safe."

Elena shrugged. "They probably are, dogs and cats can't have too many different allergies, can they?"

Drew chuckled. "Elena, anything can have different allergies. I'm allergic to gluten, so are some dogs and cats. A lot of humans, dogs, and cats are fine with it. I think different allergies are possible, but I've never seen Pebbles touch the plant."

The cat was currently looking around the living room, as if trying to figure out these changes. They seemed to be up to her standards, because she jumped up to the tallest point on the cat tower and curled up into a ball.

"Hey, she likes it!" Drew exclaimed.

"It does seem like she likes it." Elena watched the cat, or ball of fur, that was asleep now. She glanced out the porch doors. "It's a half-moon tonight. We should go sit out in the moonlight."

"Sure," Drew agreed. He grabbed a blanket off the couch, then led the way outside. He laid out the blanket on the ground.

Elena smiled at him, then lay down on the blanket. "No grass stains this time."

"Hopefully not." Drew sat down beside her and eyed her. She was acting normal, but she'd had quite a day. "How are you doing?" He asked her.

She flashed him a smile. "I'm okay," she replied, taking a deep breath. "I think I'm in shock, to be honest. Like when the investigator started explaining I just..." She shrugged. "I didn't know what to say or think. I still don't, really. Maybe I subconsciously avoid thinking about it."

Drew watched her. "It's a big thing."

Elena nodded. "A life changing thing. I thought I knew who I was. Now it's like the rug had been ripped out from under me. My dad was great growing up. I always loved spending summers in Italy with him. That was a big part of why I went to Italy after high school."

She sighed, looking up at Drew. "Now I'm being told he wasn't my biological father. Not only that, but he threatened my biological father. And that doesn't fit in at all to what I knew."

"Do you wish you'd known your biological father?" Drew asked her, laying down beside her. "That you'd gotten a chance to meet him before he passed?"

"I don't know," Elena replied slowly, her fingers playing with a piece of grass. "I haven't really thought about that, or him. I don't know anything about him. That's half of myself, I don't know anything about half of myself."

Drew was about to reply, but his phone started to ring. He pulled it out of his pocket to see who was calling. *Gabi*. "I should answer this." He told Elena.

"Hello?"

"Hey Drew." Gabi sounded tired, which made sense when it was after nine pm. "That family is back from vacation now; they can take Pebbles tomorrow. I can pick her up before you go to work."

Drew felt an overwhelming sense of shock wash over him. He'd completely forgotten that Pebbles wasn't his, that there was another foster home set up for her.

Elena rolled over and looked at Drew with a frown. "What's wrong?" She mouthed.

Drew covered the speaker of the phone with his hand. "They have another foster home for Pebbles," he explained, watching as Elena's face fell.

"Poor Pebbles. She was just getting used to living here." Elena whispered, looking towards the house.

"Drew? Did you hear me? You didn't want to foster a cat, now I'm offering you an out. Why aren't you jumping at this?" Gabi asked him.

Drew glanced towards the house, where Pebbles was presumably still sleeping on her brand-new cat tower. He thought about the box of cat food that was sitting on his counter.

"I want to keep her," he spoke aloud before he was even sure of it, but it made sense. Somehow the little cat had wormed her way into his laundry basket and his heart.

Elena's face flashed with surprise, then the biggest smile he'd ever seen.

"You want to keep her?" Gabi asked, sounding surprised. "To clarify, you mean you'll continue to foster her until she finds her forever home?"

"No. I mean I'll be her forever home. I don't know what paperwork I'll have to fill out for that, but you can get it ready and let me know what I need to do."

There was a moment of silence on the other end of the phone. "I have no idea how the cat did it. But I'll get the paperwork started, Esther will call you to finish it. There'd normally be a home study, but that can be skipped because you're already a certified foster." Gabi laughed from the other end of the phone. "Enjoy your cat, Drew."

"Thanks Gabi," Drew replied, then hung up the phone. He turned off the ringer, then buried it into his pocket again.

"You have such a soft heart buried under all those player ways," Elena told him. She lay on her belly, her hands under her face. "Maybe you don't want to admit it, but it's true."

Drew sighed. "Certain people," he glanced at the house, "And animals, seem to bring out the best in me somehow. Some make it worth having another person or animal to care for."

Elena shrugged one of her shoulders. "You seem to be pretty good at it," she replied.

Drew lay down beside her again, looking into her eyes. "About what you were saying earlier, not knowing who you are. You aren't a different person, Elena. You aren't going to change because you realized half your genes came from a different person than you thought you did. They didn't magically switch today; they've always been that way."

"You have always been Elena and you'll always be Elena. I love your energy and your bubbly personality; you can make me smile at any moment. I love that you and Pebbles seem to have a bond. I love that you were able to see right through my walls and knock them all down. I love that you love working with children as much as I do." Drew reached over and pulled Elena closer to him.

She smiled down at him. "I love that you love working with children too," Elena said with a giggle. "And I really like you. You aren't like the other guys I've met, there's something special about you. I think I found my forever home, just like Pebbles. But we are getting a different cat tree." She grimaced. "That pink color is so bright. There isn't much color in your living room and it just takes over the space. I think a white one or a green one would fit a lot better."

Drew chuckled. He could spend the rest of his life living with this amazing, bubbly woman's rants. "We can get whatever color cat tree you would like."

Elena's cheeks turned red. "That probably wasn't the moment." She pulled her hair behind her ear, then leaned down and kissed Drew. "That's what this moment is for."

Drew couldn't agree more. He pulled Elena on top of him and kissed her again as the moonlight shone down on them.

Did you love *Midwest Moonlight*? Then you should read *Any Sunrise*[1] by Kimberly R. Rose!

Alexica Luna always dreamed falling in love and finding her perfect person, but she never believed it would happen for her. After falling out of a tree at age nine, she was diagnosed with a chronic illness. It changed her life forever, and makes even daily tasks difficult. She's twenty-three years old and still lives at home, wondering when life will really start. Luckily, she has her service dog Daisy by her side and her twin brother for support.

She's always assumed that no man would be interested in her, the wheelchair usually deters them before they even ask her name. But when she meets Cameron, a man with the greenest eyes she has ever seen, Lexi starts to dream. She's shocked when he asks her to watch a

1. https://books2read.com/u/b5WwzA

2. https://books2read.com/u/b5WwzA

sunrise with him. Can her dreams become a reality? Will Any Sunrise be a pathway to forever?

Women's fiction meets romance in this sweet novella.

Also by Kimberly R. Rose

Luna Family Trilogy
Italian Sunsets
Italian Sunsets
Any Sunrise
Midwest Moonlight

About the Author

An early childhood educator turned small business woman and author; Kimberly R. Rose grew up in a small town in Wisconsin. She has loved reading since she was a child, often neglecting her schoolwork to read a book. That love for reading turned into inspiration for writing. Her favorite things in life are her faith, her family, and chocolate.

The Luna Family Trilogy is Kimberly's debut series

www.ingramcontent.com/pod-product-compliance
Lightning Source LLC
Chambersburg PA
CBHW022040170626
46808CB00003B/1297